Contents

At the Circus

May 31, 2005

Dear Grandpa,

Thank you for taking me to the circus. It was fun. I liked when the man and the big cat sat on a chair. I wish I could ride a horse like the lady in pink. I would stand up and ride.
I like the circus.
Let's go again!

Love,

Madison

 **Find It!**

Read the spelling words.
Check off the words you can find in the story.

☑ can	☑ pan	☑ man	☑ cat
☑ sat	☑ wish	☑ like	☑ lady

How many spelling words did you find? _____

Skills:

Spelling Words
with **an** and **at**

Spelling
Theme
Vocabulary

Visual Memory

Spelling Practice

Read and Spell

Copy and Spell

Spell It Again!

1. can

2. pan

3. man

4. cat

5. sat

6. wish

7. like

8. lady

What's Missing?

Skills:

Spelling Words with **an** and **at**

Spelling Theme Vocabulary

Writing Spelling Words

Using Picture Clues and Sentence Context to Identify Missing Words

Fill in the blanks to write the spelling word that names each picture.

| man | lady | cat | pan | sat | can |

c __ __

__ __ n

__ a __

p __ __

__ __ t

__ __ d __

Finish the spelling word in each sentence.

1. I w_____ I could ride.

2. We l_____ the circus.

Skills:

Spelling Words with **an** and **at**

Spelling Theme Vocabulary

Identifying Rhyming Words

Circus Rhymes

Draw a line to match the words that rhyme.

man	dish
cat	ran
wish	hat
like	bike

Write a spelling word to finish each rhyme.

Mrs. Brady
is a _____.

We had Dan
open the _____.

What does Ann
fry in the _____?

That clown _____
on his hat.

can   lady   sat   pan

A Good Start

Skills:

Capitalizing
the First Word
in a Sentence

> **A sentence begins with a capital letter.**
>
> **We went to the circus.**

Circle the sentences that begin with a capital letter.
Fix the letters that should be capitals.

1. Did you like the circus?

2. i wish we could ride the elephant.

3. the clown had a pan on his head.

4. a man rode a bike with one wheel.

5. Can they pack up the big tent?

6. The big cat was in a cage.

7. I saw a lady on a swing.

8. we sat with our friends.

Skills:

Using a Period
at the End of
a Statement

Word Order in
a Sentence

Tell Me Something

A sentence needs ending punctuation.
A sentence that tells something ends with a period. **(.)**

We see the circus tent.

Unscramble the words to make a sentence.
End each sentence with a period.

1. We circus like the

   _____

2. The clown funny is

   _____

3. flower He has a

   _____

4. It water sprays

   _____

5. wet We get

   _____

Ask Me Something

Skills:

Using a Question Mark at the End of a Question

Using Content to Complete Sentences

▶ **A sentence needs ending punctuation.**
A sentence that asks something ends with
a question mark. (?)

What did you wish for?

Fill in each blank with a word from the box. End each sentence with a question mark.

| like | chair | cat | circus | ride |

1. What is that big _____

2. Did the big cat sit on a _____

3. How many big cats are in the _____

4. Did you see the lady _____

5. Which circus act do you _____

Fun at the Circus

Ann and Ben went to the circus. Write a sentence telling what each child saw. Use a capital letter and a period.

Ann

_____

_____

_____

_____

Ben

_____

_____

_____

Write a question to ask Ann or Ben about the circus.
Use a capital letter and a question mark.

_____

_____

The Big Show

Skills:

Writing a Creative Story

Using Spelling Words in a Composition

Using Correct Capitalization and Ending Punctuation

Finish the story. Use as many spelling words as you can.

can	pan	man	cat
sat	wish	like	lady

Ann and Ben played circus. They made a tent in the yard. _____

_____

_____

_____

_____

_____

_____

_____

_____

✔ Check Your Story

○ I used a capital letter to begin each sentence.

○ I used a period or question mark at the end of each sentence.

TEST YOUR SKILLS At the Circus

My Spelling Test

Find the correct answer. Fill in the circle.

Ask someone to test you on the spelling words.

1. Which punctuation mark goes at the end of the sentence?

   We like the circus____

   ○ period (.)
   ○ question mark (?)

2. Which punctuation mark goes at the end of the sentence?

   Did you see the big cat____

   ○ period (.)
   ○ question mark (?)

3. Which sentence has the correct capital letter?

   ○ here is the circus Tent.
   ○ Where is your ticket?

1. _____

2. _____

3. _____

4. _____

5. _____

6. _____

7. _____

8. _____

4. Write the sentence correctly.

   did you wich for a kat

   _____

   _____

The Playground

Today is the first day of summer. We are going to the park. Jake's mom will take us. Jake and I are going to have fun. We like to play a ship game. We can get up onto the ship. We can jump off the ship. We can run after another ship. Will we sink it? Yes!

Find It! Read the spelling words.
Check off the words you can find in the story.

✓ up	✓ us	✓ run	✓ fun
✓ to	✓ ship	✓ jump	game

How many spelling words did you find? _____

Spelling Practice

Read and Spell	Copy and Spell	Spell It Again!
1. up	_____	_____
2. us	_____	_____
3. run	_____	_____
4. fun	_____	_____
5. jump	_____	_____
6. to	_____	_____
7. ship	_____	_____
8. game	_____	_____

Play with Puzzles

Fill in the boxes with the spelling words.

1.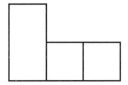

2.

3.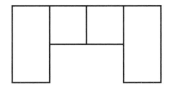

4.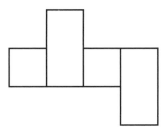

5.

6.

7.

8.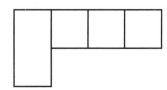

up	us	run	fun
to	ship	jump	game

Circle the spelling word in each bigger word.

funny	running	bus
cup	jumper	onto

Skills:

Spelling Words with Short **u**

Spelling Theme Vocabulary

Spelling Words in Context

Identifying Word Families

Can You Choose?

Choose the correct spelling. Write it on the line.

1. I like to gump/jump.   _____

2. How fast can you run/rum?   _____

3. We play a ship/shep game.   _____

4. We had fen/fun.   _____

5. Will you play with uss/us?   _____

6. I want to/toe swing.   _____

7. Will he play a gam/game?   _____

8. She may climb up/op.   _____

Make word families. Write the words below in the correct box.

sun	bump	pup
_____	_____	_____
_____	_____	_____

cup
bun
jump
up
run
lump

Find the Sentence

Skills:

Identifying and Writing Complete Sentences

Writing Spelling Words

▶ **A sentence has a whole thought.**

> Sentence: **The three girls jump rope.**
>
> Not a sentence: **The three girls**

Read the two groups of words. Write the group of words that makes a sentence.

1. | Play ball with me | The ball |

_____

2. | Kim and I | Kim runs to the park |

_____

3. | Jump rope with us | With me |

_____

4. | Run fun sun | It is fun to run |

_____

Skills:

Capitalizing
the First Word
in a Sentence

Use a Capital

A sentence begins with a capital letter.

Dogs play in the park.

Does the sentence begin with a capital letter? Circle **yes** or **no**.

1. We run in the park.   yes   no

2. go up the slide.   yes   no

3. we have fun in the jump house.   yes   no

4. Let's play a game.   yes   no

5. I have a ball.   yes   no

Write a sentence that goes with each picture. Use a capital
letter to begin each sentence.

_____

_____

_____

_____

_____

Capital I

> **The word I is always a capital letter.**
>
> **You and I can play a game.**

Color the 😊 if the sentence is correct. Fix the sentences that are <u>not</u> correct.

1. I like the park.

2. Ann and i can swing.

3. I like to go up.

4. Max and I ride bikes.

5. i have a blue bike.

6. May i ride your bike?

7. I can go fast.

8. You and I can race.

Writing
Complete
Sentences

Using Spelling
Words

Capitalizing
the Word **I**

What Do You Do?

Write a sentence that begins with capital **I**.

Write a sentence that tells what you like to do at the park.
Use a capital **I**.

_____

Friends Have Fun

Skills:

Writing a
Creative Story

Completing
Sentences

Using Capital I

Finish the story.

My friend's name is _____ .

We like to play _____ .

_____ .

We also like to _____

_____

_____ .

My friend and _____ have fun.

Draw a picture of yourself and your friend playing. Write
a sentence that tells about your picture.

My friend and _____ are _____

_____ .

TEST YOUR SKILLS The Playground

My Spelling Test

Find the correct answer. Fill in the circle.

1. Which one is a sentence?
   - ◯ A slide
   - ◯ A slide is fun

2. Which sentence has the correct capital letter?
   - ◯ my bike Is red.
   - ◯ Your bike is blue.

3. Which sentence has the correct capital letter?
   - ◯ Dad and I like to ride.
   - ◯ Dad and i have fun.

Ask someone to test you on the spelling words.

1. _____

2. _____

3. _____

4. _____

5. _____

6. _____

7. _____

8. _____

4. Write the sentence correctly.

   sam and i runn and jum

   _____

   _____

Note: Help your child read the story.

Fourth of July

Zack and Mia found a note on the door. They read the note. Then they asked Mom for paper. Zack made a red and white hat. Mia made red and blue flowers for her bike. Can you guess why?

Here is what the note said:

Calling All Kids!
Come to Our March!
It is in the Park.
Bring your Bike.
Be there at Noon.
You will get a flag!
You will get drinks
and snacks!

Find It! Read the spelling words.
Check off the words you can find in the story and note.

| ✓ hat | ✓ hot | ✓ sand | ✓ hand |
| ✓ red | ✓ white | ✓ blue | ✓ flag |

How many spelling words did you find? _____

Spelling Practice

Read and Spell | Copy and Spell | Spell It Again!

1. hat

2. hot

3. hand

4. sand

5. red

6. blue

7. white

8. flag

Spell It

Skills:

Spelling Words with Short **a**

Spelling Theme Vocabulary

Visual Discrimination

Writing Spelling Words

Mark an **X** on the misspelled words. Spell them correctly on the lines.

1. What color is the flage? _____

2. This box is red, whit, and blue. _____

3. The sun is hout. _____

4. Put on your blue het. _____

5. Play in the sad with me. _____

Circle each correct spelling.

1. hamd	hand	hand	hande
2. white	wite	wite	white
3. bue	bloo	blue	blue
4. hawt	haht	hot	howt

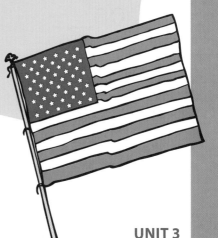

Read and Spell

Skills:

Spelling Words with Short **a**

Spelling Theme Vocabulary

Visual Memory

Using Sentence Context to Identify Missing Words

Write the spelling word that belongs in each sentence.

| hand | sand | hot | flag | white |

It is _____ tonight. We will see colors

in the sky. Put your chair on the _____.

Hold a flag in your _____. Did you hear

a big boom? There is a red and _____ star!

Wave your _____. Happy Fourth of July!

Write the last letter of each spelling word.

re___	whit__	ha___	san___
han___	blu___	ho___	fla___

Note: Read the directions to your child.

Is It a Sentence?

A sentence has a whole thought.

Sentence: **Where is my red hat?**

Not a sentence: **My red hat**

If the words make a sentence, color the **YES** star. If the words do <u>not</u> make a sentence, color the **NO** star.

1. Your hat is nice

2. Blue hat

3. The flag is blue and white

4. Dad put the chair on the sand

5. Red, white, and blue

6. The sand is hot

7. Hand sand band land

8. Please hand me a hot dog

Capital Letters

A sentence begins with a capital letter.

We saw the band march.

Circle the sentences that begin with a capital letter.
Fix the letters that should be capitals.

1. do you know what today is?

2. today is a holiday.

3. Our country has a birthday.

4. fly your flag.

5. wear red, white, and blue.

6. wear a hat in the hot sun.

7. We can hear the band play.

8. my brother plays a big drum.

Spell & Write • EMC 4537 • © Evan-Moor Corp.

Asking or Telling?

A sentence needs ending punctuation.
A sentence that tells something ends with
a period. (.)

> The band plays music.

A sentence that asks something ends with
a question mark. (?)

> What songs do they play?

Read each sentence. Draw a line to show if it is an asking
sentence or a telling sentence. The first one has been done
for you.

Do you play in a band?

I like to march.

We all have red hats.

Asking Sentence

Where is your hat?

Can you carry the flag?

Telling Sentence

Here is the flag.

Can you wave your flag?

Fun on the Fourth

Sam and Lisa had fun on the Fourth of July. Write a sentence telling what each child did. Use a capital letter and a period.

Sam

_____

_____

_____

Lisa

_____

_____

_____

Write a question asking each child about his or her day. Use a capital letter and a question mark.

Sam _____

_____

Lisa _____

_____

Holiday Fun

Skills:

Writing a
Creative Story

Using Spelling
Words in a
Composition

Using Correct
Capitalization
and Ending
Punctuation

What do you like to do on the Fourth of July? Write about it. Use as many spelling words as you can.

hat	hot	hand	sand
red	blue	white	flag

_____

_____

_____

_____

_____

_____

_____

_____

✓ Check Your Story

⭕ I used a capital letter to begin each sentence.

⭕ I used a period or question mark at the end of each sentence.

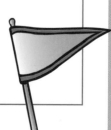

TEST YOUR SKILLS Fourth of July

My Spelling Test

Find the correct answer. Fill in the circle.

1. Which punctuation mark goes at the end of the sentence?

   Did you march with the band___

   ○ period (.)
   ○ question mark (?)

2. Which one is a sentence?

   ○ The white sand
   ○ The sand is hot

3. Which sentence has the correct capital letter?

   ○ This hat is too big for me.
   ○ my Red hat is just right.

Ask someone to test you on the spelling words.

1. _____

2. _____

3. _____

4. _____

5. _____

6. _____

7. _____

8. _____

4. Write the sentence correctly.

   my flag is rad, white, and blu

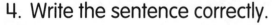

_____

_____

Story of the Year

The story of the year goes like this:

In the **spring**, baby birds and lambs are born. The days get warmer. Little plants begin to grow.

Summer brings long days of hot sun. The garden is full of flowers and bees. We go to the beach.

In the **fall**, leaves turn yellow, red, and brown. They fall from the trees. We rake them up.

Winter comes and brings the cold. A bear sleeps. The lake has a cover of ice. We have fun in the snow. We make tracks.

Year after year, the story goes on. First spring comes, then summer, fall, and winter.

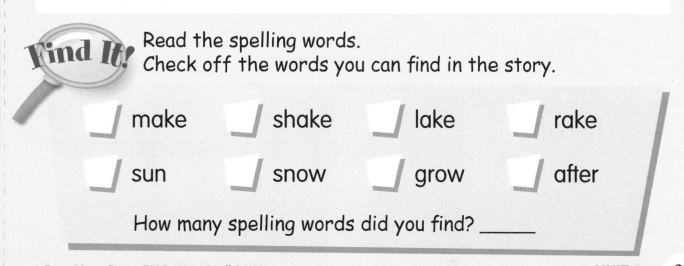

Find It!
Read the spelling words.
Check off the words you can find in the story.

☑ make	☑ shake	☑ lake	☑ rake
☑ sun	☑ snow	☑ grow	☑ after

How many spelling words did you find? _____

Spelling Practice

Read and Spell	Copy and Spell	Spell It Again!
1. make	_____	_____
2. shake	_____	_____
3. lake	_____	_____
4. rake	_____	_____
5. sun	_____	_____
6. snow	_____	_____
7. grow	_____	_____
8. after	_____	_____

Note: Read the directions to your child.

Write Your Words

Skills:

Spelling Words with **ake** and **ow**

Spelling Theme Vocabulary

Writing Spelling Words

Visual Memory and Discrimination

Spelling Words in Context

Fill in the boxes with the spelling words.

after	sun	snow	grow

1.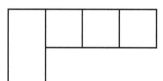

3.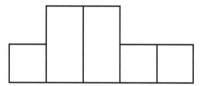

2.

4.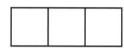

Finish the missing spelling words.

shake	rake	lake	make

1. Please hand me the r_____.

2. Let's m_____ a big pile of leaves.

3. I can sh_____ an apple off the tree.

4. It is too cold to swim in the l_____.

© Evan-Moor Corp. • EMC 4537 • Spell & Write   UNIT 4   **35**

Choose One

Skills:

Spelling Words with **ake** and **ow**

Spelling Theme Vocabulary

Spelling Words in Context

Identifying Word Families

Choose the correct spelling. Write it on the line.

1. The sum/sun is hot. _____

2. Dad will take us to the lake/lak. _____

3. We can mack/make a sand pile. _____

4. See it groo/grow. _____

5. I will sake/shake off the sand. _____

6. Alan has a pail and a rake/roke. _____

7. The sand is as white as snow/snoe. _____

8. Let's play aftr/after we swim. _____

Make word families. Write the words below in the correct box.

sun   grow   shake   snow   lake   run

low	fun	make
_____	_____	_____
_____	_____	_____

Nouns Name Things

Some words name things. These words are called nouns.

The lady has a blue hat.

Color each apple that names something.

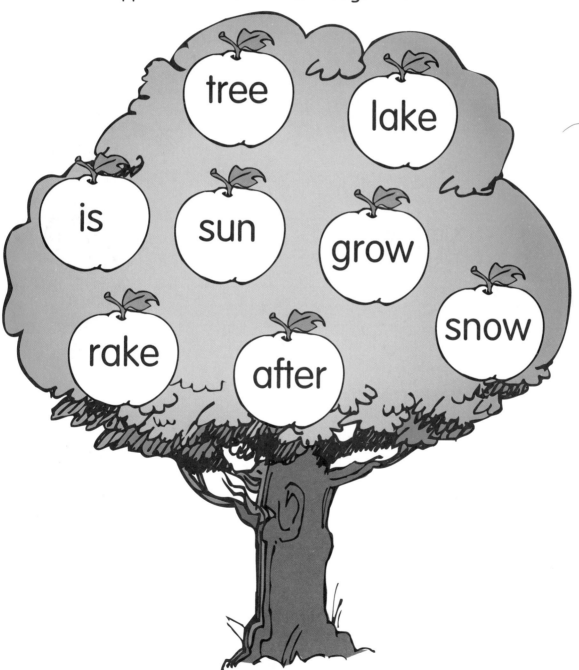

Note: Read the directions to your child.

Skills:

Using **'s**
to Show
Possession

Summer Fun

**When something belongs to one person,
add 's to the name of the person.**

We swim in Amy's pool.

Draw a line to show to whom each thing belongs.

Meg's ●
kite

Kim's ●
T-shirt

Tom's ●
ball

Ben's ●
boat

Spell & Write • EMC 4537 • © Evan-Moor Corp.

Winter Fun

Write the name to show who owns each thing. Use 's.

1. Matt has skates.  _____ skates	2. Jan has boots.  _____ boots
3. Dan has a hat.  _____ hat	4. Maria has mittens.  _____ mittens
5. Ana has a sled.  _____ sled	6. Marco has a scarf.  _____ scarf

Skills:

Writing Creative Sentences

Identifying Nouns

Around the Year

Finish each sentence to tell about the season. Circle the nouns in your sentences.

Winter

In the winter, I

_____

_____ .

Spring

In the spring, I

_____

_____ .

Summer

In the summer, I

_____

_____ .

Fall

In the fall, I

_____

_____ .

Spell & Write • EMC 4537 • © Evan-Moor Corp.

Time of Year

Skills:

Writing a
Poem

Using **'s**
to Show
Possession

Finish the poem. Fill in the name of the season.

| winter | spring | fall | summer |

I like spring.

I like _____'s rain.

I like _____'s soft, quiet rain.

I like summer.

I like _____'s sun.

I like _____'s hot, hot sun.

I like fall.

I like _____'s colors.

I like _____'s red and yellow leaves.

I like winter.

I like _____'s snow.

I like _____'s white, white snow.

TEST YOUR SKILLS — Story of the Year

My Spelling Test

Find the correct answer. Fill in the circle.

1. Which one is a naming word? (noun)
   - ○ swim
   - ○ lake

2. Which sentence shows that Ana owns something?
   - ○ These are Anas mittens.
   - ○ These are Ana's boots.

3. Which one tells to whom something belongs?
   - ○ Lee's bike
   - ○ red bike

Ask someone to test you on the spelling words.

1. _____

2. _____

3. _____

4. _____

5. _____

6. _____

7. _____

8. _____

4. Write the sentence correctly.

the sum will mak Dans tree gro

_____

_____

Good Morning!

Wake up! It's morning. What do you **see**?
  The sun in the sky
  And birds in a tree.

Wake up! It's morning. What do you **hear**?
  Someone is singing
  A song soft and clear.

Wake up! It's morning. What do you **hold**?
  The covers around me
  To keep out the cold.

Wake up! It's morning. What do you **smell**?
  Someone is frying
  An egg, I can tell.

Wake up! It's morning. What do you **eat**?
  Warm oats and cold milk,
  And berries so sweet.

Find It! Read the spelling words.
Check off the words you can find in the story.

| ✓ we | ✓ me | ✓ tree | ✓ see |
| ✓ hear | ✓ hold | ✓ smell | ✓ eat |

How many spelling words did you find? _____

Skills:

Spelling Words
with Long **e**

Spelling
Theme
Vocabulary

Visual Memory

Spelling Practice

Read and Spell	Copy and Spell	Spell It Again!
1. we	_____	_____
2. me	_____	_____
3. tree	_____	_____
4. see	_____	_____
5. hear	_____	_____
6. hold	_____	_____
7. smell	_____	_____
8. eat	_____	_____

See and Write

Skills:

Spelling Words
with Long **e**

Spelling
Theme
Vocabulary

Visual Memory

Practice your spelling words. Write the missing letters.

we	me	tree
__ e	__ e	__ __ ee
w __	m __	tr __ __
__ __	__ __	__ __ __ __

see		eat
__ ee		__ __ t
s __ __		ea __
__ __ __		__ __ __

hear	hold	smell
__ ear	__ old	__ __ ell
h __ __ __	h __ __ __	sm __ __ __
__ __ __ __	__ __ __ __	__ __ __ __ __

Skills:

Spelling Words with Long **e**

Spelling Theme Vocabulary

Spelling Words in Context

Visual Discrimination

Can You See It?

Choose the correct spelling. Write it on the line.

1. My new glasses help me/mi read. _____

2. Can you sey/see the pictures? _____

3. I will hould/hold the book for you. _____

4. Now wee/we can read together. _____

we	me	tree	see
hear	hold	smell	eat

Circle the spelling word in each bigger word.

meet   treetop   behold   seeds

hearing   smelly   beater   sweet

Find the Verbs

▶ Some words tell what is happening. These words are called verbs.

We smell the popcorn.
(What is happening)

Color the verbs.

hear

eat

see

egg

hold

tree

smell

we

Skills:

Using
Pronouns in
Context

Using Pronouns

Some words take the place of names. These words are called pronouns.

Rose likes ice cream.
She could eat it every day.

Dan and I like to dance.
We hear the music.

Use a word from the box to complete each sentence.

he	she	we	me

1. _____ are glad the sun is shining.

2. The birds seem to sing to _____.

3. My teddy bear looks like _____ is happy, too.

4. I can hear Dad. _____ is calling to _____.

5. What will _____ eat for breakfast?

6. Mom is cooking. _____ is making eggs.

I or Me?

Skills:

Using
Pronouns **I**
and **Me**

▶ Use **I** when you are the person doing something.

> **I** bake cookies with Mother.

Use **me** when something happens to you.

> Mother gave **me** a cookie.

Fill in the blanks with **I** or **me**.

1. _____ have fun cooking.

2. Father and _____ make cookies.

3. He lets _____ help.

4. _____ put in flour and sugar.

5. Father helps _____ mix the batter.

6. _____ put the cookies on a plate.

7. Father gives _____ a taste.

8. _____ think they are good.

Skills:

Writing
Complete
Sentences

Using the
Pronoun **I**

Using My Senses

Write a sentence about something you like to see, hear, touch, smell, and taste. Use **I** in your sentences.

see

_____

_____

hear

_____

_____

touch

_____

_____

smell

_____

_____

taste

_____

_____

A Funny Noise

Skills:

Writing a
Creative Story

Using Spelling
Words in a
Composition

Finish the story. Use as many spelling words as you can.

we	me	tree	see
hear	hold	smell	eat

One day, I heard a funny noise. It was outside.

I went to look. I saw _____

_____

_____

_____

_____

_____

_____

_____

✔ **Check Your Story**

◯ I used complete sentences.

◯ I used the words **I** and **me** correctly.

Good Morning!

My Spelling Test

Find the correct answer. Fill in the circle.

1. Which word tells what is happening?
   - ○ eat
   - ○ tree

2. Which pronoun goes in the blank?

   Sam gave _____ his book.
   - ○ I
   - ○ me

3. Which pronoun goes in the blank?

   Jenny can smell the flower.

   _____ likes flowers.
   - ○ We
   - ○ She

Ask someone to test you on the spelling words.

1. _____

2. _____

3. _____

4. _____

5. _____

6. _____

7. _____

8. _____

4. Write the sentence correctly.

   wee sea an apple on the tre

   _____

   _____

Spell & Write • EMC 4537 • © Evan-Moor Corp.

Sing a Song

A song needs notes. Hum a song you know. Can you hear the notes go up and down?

A song needs a beat. You can clap the beat of a song. Clap one–two–three–four!

Some songs have words. The words may be **happy**, **silly**, **sad**, or **nice**. Words help you feel the song.

So sing your song the way you feel it!

Find It!

Read the spelling words.
Check off the words you can find in the story.

☑ so	☑ no	☑ note	☑ home
☑ do	☑ you	☑ nice	☑ sing

How many spelling words did you find? _____

Spelling Practice

Read and Spell	Copy and Spell	Spell It Again!
1. so	_____	_____
2. no	_____	_____
3. note	_____	_____
4. home	_____	_____
5. do	_____	_____
6. you	_____	_____
7. nice	_____	_____
8. sing	_____	_____

Can You Spell It?

Skills:

Spelling Words with Long **o**

Spelling Theme Vocabulary

Visual Discrimination

Writing Spelling Words

Mark an **X** on the misspelled words. Spell them correctly on the lines.

1. How doo we sound? _____

2. Will Troy singe with us? _____

3. He has a nise voice. _____

4. Play this not. _____

5. Can yu play a tune? _____

Fill in the boxes with the spelling words.

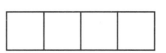

home   nice   sing   you

1.

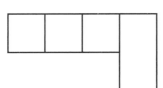

3.

2.

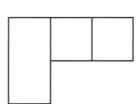

4.

Rhyme Time

Circle two words in each row that rhyme with the first word.

1.	**sing**	bring	song	ring
2.	**note**	not	vote	boat
3.	**nice**	mice	twice	size
4.	**so**	no	to	go
5.	**you**	do	blue	snow
6.	**no**	too	show	so
7.	**home**	foam	Rome	come
8.	**do**	moo	no	you

Write a spelling word to finish each rhyme.

Does the king

Like to _____?

He sang it twice,

It was _____.

Spell & Write • EMC 4537 • © Evan-Moor Corp.

Is It a Sentence?

A sentence has a whole thought.

Sentence: **It is fun to play music.**

Not a sentence: **To play music**

If the words make a sentence, color the happy face.
If the words do <u>not</u> make a sentence, color the sad face.

1. The band

2. We play in a band

3. We keep the beat

4. With two sticks

5. I tap with the sticks

6. So no so no so

7. Ring the bell

8. Tap the triangle

Skills:

Using
Capital **I**

Looking for I

Circle the sentences that have a capital **I**.
Fix the sentences that do <u>not</u> have a capital **I**.

1. Rita and I have fun.

2. i turn on the radio.

3. I like to sing and dance.

4. When the music plays, i listen.

5. I show Rita the steps.

6. She and i practice at home.

7. i can snap my fingers.

8. Rita and I can teach you, too.

We or Us?

► Use **we** when you and other people do something.

> **We** learn the tune.

Use **us** when something happens to you and other people.

> Mr. Bell will teach **us** a song.

Fill in the each blank with **we** or **us**.

1. _____ go to music class.

2. _____ learn about notes.

3. Some of _____ sing high notes.

4. Two of _____ play the bells.

5. _____ learn to sing together.

6. Next week, _____ are in a show.

7. In the show _____ will sing and dance.

8. Will you sing with _____?

Skills:

Using Capital **I**

My Music

Do you play or sing music? What would you like to play? What would you like to sing? Write about it. Use some of your spelling words.

_____

_____

_____

_____

_____

_____

Draw a picture of yourself making music.

✓ **Check Your Story**

○ I used complete sentences.

○ I used capital **I** correctly.

My Top Ten

Make a list of songs you know. Draw a star by the song you like best.

1. _____

2. _____

3. _____

4. _____

5. _____

6. _____

7. _____

8. _____

9. _____

10. _____

Sing your song for someone.

TEST YOUR SKILLS Sing a Song

My Spelling Test

Find the correct answer. Fill in the circle.

Ask someone to test you on the spelling words.

1. Which one is a sentence?
   - ○ He plays a nice tune
   - ○ A note

2. Which word goes in the blank?

   _____ shake the bells.
   - ○ Us
   - ○ We

3. Which sentence has the correct capital letter?
   - ○ Travis and i like to sing.
   - ○ You and I like to dance.

1. _____

2. _____

3. _____

4. _____

5. _____

6. _____

7. _____

8. _____

4. Write the sentence correctly.

   doo us hum or sinng the nots

   _____

   _____

Be Safe

At school, Min and Adam learned how to be safe. A firefighter came to visit. He showed the children his gear and his truck. He told them how to stay safe. He gave them a list. It has a good rule to remember. If you see a fire, dial 9-1-1. Min and Adam like to play with toy fire trucks. They may want to fight fires one day.

Find It! Read the spelling words.
Check off the words you can find in the story.

☑ day	☑ may	☑ stay	☑ play
☑ stop	☑ look	☑ rule	☑ safe

How many spelling words did you find? _____

Skills:

Spelling Words
with **ay**

Spelling
Theme
Vocabulary

Visual Memory

Spelling Practice

Read and Spell | **Copy and Spell** | **Spell It Again!**

1. day

2. may

3. stay

4. play

5. stop

6. look

7. rule

8. safe

Write Your Words

Skills:

Spelling Words with **ay**

Writing Spelling Words

Visual Memory and Discrimination

Fill in the boxes with the spelling words.

| day | may | stay | play |

1.
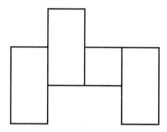

3.
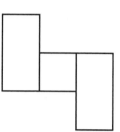

2.
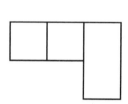

4.
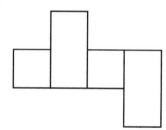

Finish the missing spelling words.

1. St_____ before you cross the street.

2. Be sure to l_____ both ways.

3. That is a good r_____ to follow.

4. It's up to you to be sa_____.

Skills:

Using Sentence Context to Identify Missing Words

Writing Spelling Words

Using Vowel Sounds

Play It Safe

Fill in the missing words.

| may | stay | day | play |

1. Will you _____ and play?

2. Do not _____ in the street.

3. You _____ get hurt.

4. Have a safe _____.

Write letters in the blanks to make spelling words.

| oo | u | o | ay | a |

d_____	m_____
st_____p	r_____le
s_____fe	st_____
l_____k	pl_____

What Happened?

> Some words tell what is happening or what already happened. These words are called verbs.
>
> ### We see the red light.
> (What is happening)
>
> ### We waited to cross the street.
> (What already happened)

Fill in the blanks with words from the box. Circle the words that tell what happened.

do	stay	look	stop
play	fell	called	came

1. We try to _____ safe.

2. We know what to _____.

3. We do not _____ in the street.

4. We _____ at every corner.

5. We always _____ both ways.

6. One time, I _____ down in the street.

7. I _____ to my friend for help.

8. She _____ right away.

Bike Safety

Use is with one and are with more than one.

That is a nice bike.

Our bikes are the same color.

Fill in each blank with **is** or **are**.

1. Here _____ my new bike.

2. There _____ three bikes in our family.

3. What _____ the bike rule?

4. It _____ good to look for cars.

5. Two kids _____ at the stop sign.

6. This _____ a helmet.

7. It _____ safe to wear a helmet when you ride.

8. Our helmets _____ purple.

Important to Know

▶ Use they when several people do something.
Use them when something happens to several people.

> They got lost in the store.
>
> Mother couldn't find them.

Fill in each blank with **they** or **them**.

1. _____ asked the guard for help.

2. The guard helped _____.

3. What did _____ tell the guard?

4. _____ knew their mother's name.

5. Mother was so happy to see _____.

6. Do _____ know their phone number?

7. Tell _____ to learn their address.

Keep Safe

Skills:

Writing
Complete
Sentences

Using
Picture Clues

Identifying
Verbs

Tell how each child is being safe.

Circle a verb in each of the sentences you wrote.

School Rules

Skills:

Writing a
Creative Story

Using Spelling
Words in a
Composition

Read the safety rule. Write a story about a boy who didn't follow the rule. How many spelling words can you use in your story?

Rule: Walk, don't run in school.

day	stop	may	look
stay	rule	play	safe

_____

_____

_____

_____

_____

_____

_____

✔ Check Your Story

◯ I used complete sentences.

◯ I used capital letters correctly.

◯ I used punctuation marks.

Note: Read the assessment questions to your child.

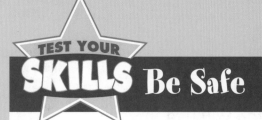

TEST YOUR SKILLS Be Safe

My Spelling Test

Find the correct answer. Fill in the circle.

1. Which word tells what is happening? (verb)
    ○ look
    ○ them

2. Which word goes in the blank?

    The fire _____ out.
    ○ is
    ○ are

3. Which word goes in the blank?

    Did _____ stop at the stop sign?
    ○ them
    ○ they

Ask someone to test you on the spelling words.

1. _____

2. _____

3. _____

4. _____

5. _____

6. _____

7. _____

8. _____

4. Write the sentence correctly.

    the rool says to stopp and looke

    _____

    _____

Spell & Write • EMC 4537 • © Evan-Moor Corp.

Away We Go!

How do you get from place to place?

Do you live in the city?
In the city, you might go by bus,
by train, or by car. You might
walk or ride a bike.

Do you live in the country?
In the country, you might
go by truck, by jeep, or
by tractor.

Do you want to go far, far away?
Do you want to float on the wind?
Take a hot-air balloon ride!

There are many ways to get from place to place.

Find It! Read the spelling words.
Check off the words you can find in the story.

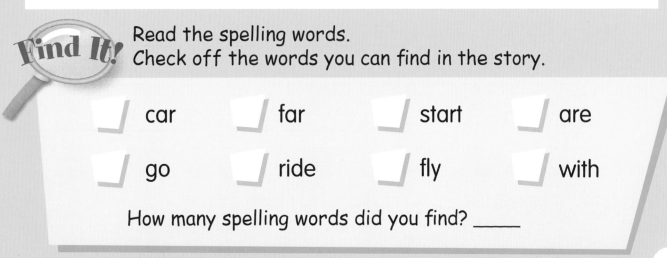

| | car | | far | | start | | are |
| | go | | ride | | fly | | with |

How many spelling words did you find? _____

Spelling Practice

Read and Spell	Copy and Spell	Spell It Again!

1. car

2. far

3. start

4. are

5. go

6. ride

7. fly

8. with

A Car Trip

Skills:

Using Sentence Context to Identify Missing Words

Writing Spelling Words

Visual Memory

Fill in the missing spelling words.

far	ride	go	start	are	car

1. We _____ going on a trip.

2. Dad will pack the_____.

3. We are ready to _____!

4. Carly and I can _____ in the back.

5. Mom will _____ the car.

6. How _____ is it to the ocean?

Circle the words that are spelled correctly.

1. with   witt

2. stort   start

3. fly   fliy

4. ryde   ride

Skills:

Spelling Words with R-Controlled Vowel **ar**

Spelling Theme Vocabulary

Visual Memory

Ride with Me

Practice your spelling words. Write the missing letters.

car	are	ride
___ ar	___ ___ e	___ ide
c ___ ___	ar ___	r ___ ___ e
___ ___ ___	___ ___ ___	___ ___ ___ ___

far		fly
___ ar		___ ___ y
f ___ ___		fl ___
___ ___ ___		___ ___ ___

start	go	with
___ ___ art	___ o	___ ith
st ___ ___ t	g ___	wi ___ ___
___ ___ ___ ___ ___	___ ___	___ ___ ___ ___

Let's Lift Off!

> **Verbs** tell what is happening or what already happened.
>
> We see the rocket.
> The rocket landed.

Read each sentence. Write the word
that tells what is happening or what already happened. (verb)

1. We ride in a rocket. _____

2. See the rocket fly high. _____

3. It went to the moon. _____

4. Our rocket landed. _____

5. I walked on the moon. _____

6. Next, we go to Mars. _____

7. I start the rockets. _____

8. The ship goes home. _____

9. We see the Earth. _____

Skills:

Identifying
Contractions

Contraction Action

A contraction is a short way to write two words.

Do not **go far.**   It is **a big ship.**
Don't **go far.**   It's **a big ship.**

Draw a line to match each contraction with the two words used to make it.

can't	they have
you'll	he is
they've	can not
she's	you will
he's	we are
I'm	let us
we're	I am
let's	she is

More Contractions

Skills:

Writing Contractions Using an Apostrophe

▶ The apostrophe takes the place of a letter or letters. A contraction uses an apostrophe. (')

does not = doesn't

Rewrite each sentence using a contraction. Use an apostrophe.

| We'll | Where's | it's | They're | don't |

1. Where is that boat going?

   _____

2. I think it is a fishing boat.

   _____

3. We will sail this way.

   _____

4. I do not see land.

   _____

5. They are going fishing.

   _____

Up We Go!

Pretend you are taking a hot-air balloon ride. Look down. What do you see? Write about it. How many spelling words can you use?

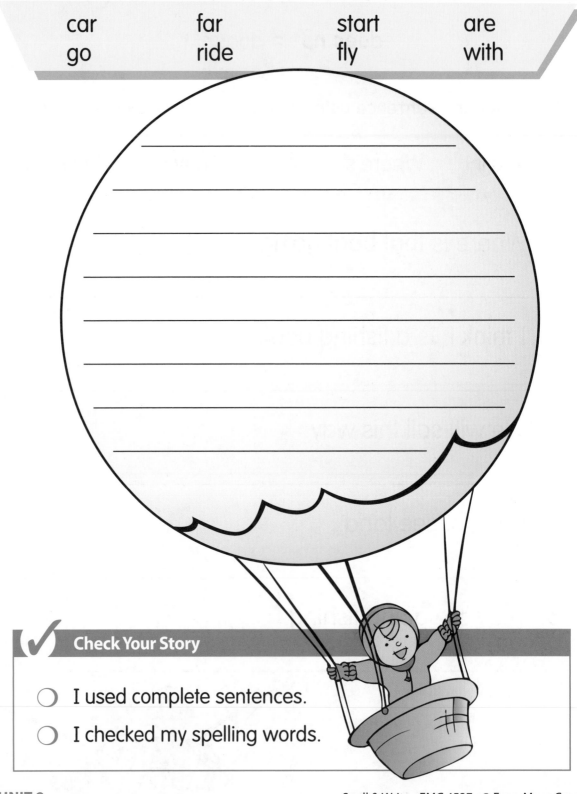

| car | far | start | are |
| go | ride | fly | with |

✓ Check Your Story

○ I used complete sentences.

○ I checked my spelling words.

Train, Car, or Plane?

Think about a place you went. Answer the questions using complete sentences. Then draw a picture to show how you got there.

1. Where did you go?

   _____

   _____

2. Who went with you?

   _____

   _____

3. How did you get there?

   _____

   _____

Draw a picture.

TEST YOUR SKILLS — Away We Go!

My Spelling Test

Find the correct answer. Fill in the circle.

1. Which word tells what is happening? (verb)
   - ○ ride
   - ○ car

2. Which word is the contraction for **have not**?
   - ○ have
   - ○ haven't

3. Which word is the contraction for **do not**?
   - ○ didn't
   - ○ don't

Ask someone to test you on the spelling words.

1. _____

2. _____

3. _____

4. _____

5. _____

6. _____

7. _____

8. _____

4. Write the sentence correctly.

   Lets goe for a rid in the care

   _____

   _____

Note: Help your child read the story.

On the Farm

The rooster crows, "Cock-a-doodle-do!" It's time for the farm animals to wake up. It's time for the farmer to wake up, too. The farmer eats fresh eggs for breakfast. Now it is time to walk down to the barn. Twinkle, the brown cow, waits for him. She knows it's milking time. The cats that live in the barn want to help. They want some of Twinkle's fresh milk, too!

Find It! Read the spelling words.
Check off the words you can find in the story.

| ☑ cow | ☑ now | ☑ down | ☑ town |
| ☑ brown | ☑ farm | ☑ barn | ☑ help |

How many spelling words did you find? _____

Spelling Practice

Read and Spell	Copy and Spell	Spell It Again!
1. cow	_____	_____
2. now	_____	_____
3. down	_____	_____
4. town	_____	_____
5. brown	_____	_____
6. farm	_____	_____
7. barn	_____	_____
8. help	_____	_____

See and Spell

Skills:

Spelling Words with **ow**

Spelling Theme Vocabulary

Visual Discrimination

Choose the correct spelling. Write it on the line.

1. Will you hepp/help us feed the chickens? _____

2. The feed is in the bern/barn. _____

3. Nowe/Now we get the eggs. _____

4. Then we can drive to town/tone. _____

Circle two words in each row that rhyme with the first word.

1. **down**	gown	town	done
2. **farm**	charm	ham	harm
3. **brown**	brow	clown	crown
4. **now**	low	cow	how

Skills:

Spelling Words with **ow**

Spelling Theme Vocabulary

Spelling Words in Context

Visual Discrimination

Our Farm

Mark an **X** on the misspelled words. Spell them correctly on the lines.

1. Sam lives on a fram. _____

2. Sam has a kow. _____

3. We will go done to see his cow. _____

4. She is broun with a white face. _____

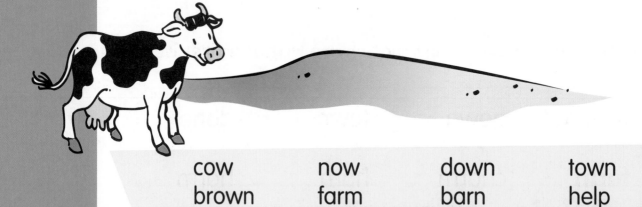

cow	now	down	town
brown	farm	barn	help

Circle the spelling word in each bigger word.

brownies   helper

farmhouse   barnyard

cowgirl   uptown

known   downstairs

Finish the Sentences

Skills:

Using Sentence Context to Identify Missing Words

Using Ending Punctuation

A sentence that tells something ends with a period.(.)

We are going to the farm.

A sentence that asks something ends with a question mark. (?)

Would you like to visit a farm?

Fill in the blanks with words from the box below. End each sentence with a period or a question mark.

1. Our friends live on a _____

2. Have you ever been inside a red _____

3. They have horses, pigs, and a _____

4. Do you live on a farm or in _____

5. Is your horse black or _____

6. Let's go to town _____

| farm | now | barn | town | brown | cow |

Skills:

Writing
Contractions
Using an
Apostrophe

Contractions

A contraction is a short way to write two words.
A contraction uses an apostrophe. (')

We will plant the beans.
We'll plant corn, too.

Write the contraction for each pair of words. Use an apostrophe.

1. you will _____

2. I am _____

3. here is _____

4. you are _____

5. is not _____

6. we have _____

7. what is _____

8. did not _____

Is and Are

▶ Use is with one and are with more than one.

> The pear is in the basket.
>
> The apples are in the box.

Fill in each blank with **is** or **are**.

1. Our farm _____ a fruit farm.

2. That tree _____ a pear tree.

3. The pears _____ ready to pick.

4. There _____ boxes for the pears.

5. Here _____ the pear truck.

6. The apple trees _____ over there.

7. This _____ a sweet apple.

8. The apples _____ in a basket.

Skills:

Writing Asking
Sentences

Using
Question
Marks

Farm Questions

Think of three facts you know about farms. Write each fact as a question. End each question with a question mark.

1. _____

_____

2. _____

_____

3. _____

_____

Draw a picture of a farm.

On the Farm

Skills:

Writing a
Creative Story

Write a story about a class trip to a farm. Tell what the
children saw. Use as many spelling words as you can.

cow	now	down	town
brown	farm	barn	help

_____

_____

_____

_____

_____

_____

_____

_____

✓ Check Your Story

○ I used complete sentences.

○ I used a period or question mark at the end
   of each sentence.

TEST YOUR SKILLS On the Farm

My Spelling Test

Find the correct answer. Fill in the circle.

Ask someone to test you on the spelling words.

1. Which punctuation mark goes at the end of the sentence?

   Do you live on a farm____

   ○ period (.)
   ○ question mark (?)

2. Which word is the contraction for **did not**?

   ○ don't
   ○ didn't

3. Which word goes in the sentence?

   These _____ the pears we picked.

   ○ is
   ○ are

1. _____

2. _____

3. _____

4. _____

5. _____

6. _____

7. _____

8. _____

4. Write the sentence correctly.

   does the brawn kow stay in the bran

   _____

   _____

Note: Help your child read the story.

Pet Show

We are having a pet show today.
Nick will bring a little bunny.
It is black and white.

Sierra will bring her kitten.
The kitten has a bell that
always tells where she is.

I will bring my funny puppy
to the pet show. His name
is Tucker. I am teaching
Tucker to sit. He is happy
when he gets a treat. He
wags his tail and licks
my face.

Can you come to our pet show?

Find It! Read the spelling words.
Check off the words you can find in the story.

- ☐ funny
- ☐ bunny
- ☐ puppy
- ☐ happy
- ☐ little
- ☐ kitten
- ☐ pet
- ☐ my

How many spelling words did you find? _____

Skills:

Spelling Theme Vocabulary

Visual Memory

Spelling Words with Double Consonants

Spelling Words That End with **y**

Read and Spell	Copy and Spell	Spell It Again!
1. funny	_____	_____
2. bunny	_____	_____
3. puppy	_____	_____
4. happy	_____	_____
5. little	_____	_____
6. kitten	_____	_____
7. pet	_____	_____
8. my	_____	_____

Pet Puzzles

Fill in the boxes with the spelling words.

funny	bunny	puppy	happy
little	kitten	pet	my

1.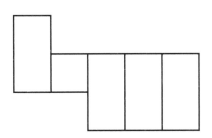

5.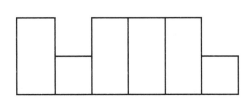

2.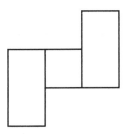

6.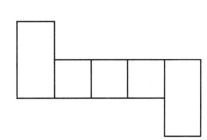

3.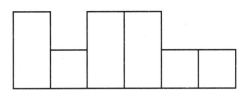

7.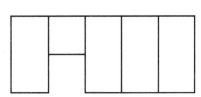

4.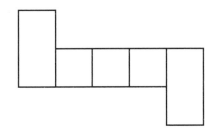

8.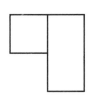

Choose a Word

Choose the correct spelling. Write it on the line.

1. My kittn/kitten likes to play. _____

2. It is a happy/happey cat. _____

3. Does your bunne/bunny eat carrots? _____

4. What kind of pat/pet would you like? _____

5. This is my/mi frog. _____

6. Your puppy/pupy is smart. _____

7. I have five litel/little fish. _____

8. A dog with a hat is funny/funey. _____

Fill in the missing letters to make spelling words.

n	p	t

ha __ __ y	li __ __ le	pu __ __ y
fu __ __ y	ki __ __ en	bu __ __ y

Correct Capitals

Skills:

Capitalizing the First Word in a Sentence

> **A sentence begins with a capital letter.**
>
> **My dog takes me for a walk.**

Circle the sentences that begin with a capital letter.
Fix the letters that should be capitals.

1. My kitten is a good pet.

2. it likes to play with a ball of string.

3. the funny kitten got twisted up.

4. I had to help it.

5. now my kitten is happy.

6. what does your puppy play with?

7. Does the bunny like to play?

8. Every pet needs love.

Skills:

Capitalizing Names of People, Pets, and Specific Places and Things

Capitals for Names

The names of people, pets, and specific places and things begin with a capital letter.

April has two horses named Hanna and Harry.

She rides at Oak Tree Ranch.

Use red to circle the names of people and pets. Use blue to circle the names of special places and things.

1. Today the Texas State Fair begins.

2. April will take her horse.

3. She will brush Hanna's coat.

4. Carlos comes from Red River Ranch.

5. Carlos will ride in the ring.

6. He will ride a horse named Rex.

7. April and Carlos want a blue ribbon.

8. The blue ribbon says "First Place."

Pick Your Pronoun

▶ **Some words take the place of names. These words are called pronouns.**

Bunny Boo **likes to hop around the yard.**

She **hops in the grass.**

Fill in the blanks with words from the box below. Replace the underlined words.

1. My <u>dog</u> Trotter is a fast runner.

   _____ likes to play chase.

2. My <u>kittens</u> are Pepper and Spice.

   _____ look alike.

3. <u>Tina and I</u> have pet birds.

   The birds sing to _____.

4. <u>Mom and I</u> want a puppy.

   _____ want a little one.

we	he	us	they

Pet Report

Answer the questions using complete sentences. Use a capital letter at the beginning of each sentence.

1. What pet would you choose?

   _____

   _____

2. Why would you choose that pet?

   _____

   _____

3. What is a good name for your pet?

   _____

Draw a picture of your pet.

Note: Read the directions to your child.

Make a Poster

Skills:

Creative
Writing

Writing
Information

Making a
Poster

The children are having a pet show. Make a sign for the show.
Decorate your sign. How many spelling words can you use?

| funny | bunny | puppy | happy |
| little | kitten | pet | my |

Pet Show

My Spelling Test

Find the correct answer. Fill in the circle.

Ask someone to test you on the spelling words.

1. Which sentence has the correct capital letter?
   - ○ the pet show is today.
   - ○ I like the kittens.

2. Which sentence has the correct capital letters?
   - ○ My dog went to Red's Puppy School.
   - ○ now clifford knows how to sit.

3. Which pronoun goes in the blank?

   Luke has a new kitten.
   _____ calls it Penny.
   - ○ He
   - ○ They

1. _____

2. _____

3. _____

4. _____

5. _____

6. _____

7. _____

8. _____

4. Write the sentence correctly.

   mi littel bunney is named sunny

   _____

   _____

Note: Help your child read the story.

Family Night

I love family night at my house. It is the same every week. We all help with dinner. Our dog Sam knows something is up. After dinner, we all wash the dishes. Then we choose a board game. My brother and I choose a game. We have fun playing games together. My mother and father play, too. We all have fun on family night.

Find It! Read the spelling words.
Check off the words you can find in the story.

- [ ] game
- [ ] name
- [ ] bake
- [ ] family
- [ ] mother
- [ ] father
- [ ] brother
- [ ] sister

How many spelling words did you find? _____

Spelling Practice

Read and Spell

Copy and Spell

Spell It Again!

1. game

2. name

3. bake

4. family

5. mother

6. father

7. sister

8. brother

Word Search

Circle each spelling word.

game	name	bake	family
mother	father	sister	brother

sisternamebrothergamemotherfamilybakefather

gamenamemotherfatherbrotherfamilysisterbake

bakenamebrothergamefathersisterfamilymother

Circle the words that are spelled correctly.

1. muther   mother

2. name   nume

3. father   fathr

4. sistre   sister

5. gamm   game

6. family   famile

7. brother   bruther

8. backe   bake

Skills:

Spelling Words
with Long **a**

Spelling
Theme
Vocabulary

Visual Memory

Word Study

Fill in the spelling word for each sentence.

| game | bake | mother | brother |

1. Jim is my little _____.

2. My _____ asked me to watch him.

3. Let's play a _____.

4. Mother will _____ us some cookies.

Add the missing letters to make spelling words.

| me | er | ke | ly |

1. fath____   5. moth____

2. sist____   6. broth____

3. fami____   7. ga____

4. na____   8. ba____

Names Have Capitals

Skills:

Capitalizing Names of People, Pets, and Specific Places and Things

▶ The names of people, pets, and specific places and things begin with a capital letter.

> Emily is going to New York.
>
> She will take her dog Red.
>
> Her dad will drive the Ford truck.

Use red to circle the names of people and pets. Use blue to circle the names of special places and things.

1. Mike and Tony are brothers.

2. They live in Ohio.

3. Mike goes to Red Hill School.

4. Nemo is the name of Tony's fish.

5. He got the fish at Dave's Dive.

6. Their family is going to Mexico.

7. I will feed Nemo.

8. He likes Fine Fish Flakes.

Skills:

Identifying
and
Writing Nouns

Write the Nouns

Some words name things. These words are called nouns.

Harry read a story about a family.

Choose the noun. Write it in the sentence.

1. This is a good _____ to read.	**book** **sing**
2. My father reads it to us in _____.	**sleep** **bed**
3. I like the magic _____.	**look** **skunk**
4. The skunk's _____ is Miss Sweet.	**name** **hear**
5. The skunk takes a _____.	**hide** **bath**
6. That is a funny _____.	**story** **think**

Family Names

▶ **When something belongs to one person, add 's to the name of the person.**

Have you seen Uncle Ted's hat?

Who owns what? Write the name you choose in each blank. Use 's.

Aunt Beth	Mother	Grandpa	Ben	Leo
Mrs. Smart	Anna	Uncle Jay	Roy	

1. We are going to _____ farm.

2. I will ride _____ horse.

3. My brother can feed _____ goats.

4. We will eat _____ cake.

5. We can help pick _____ beans.

6. We will smell _____ flowers.

7. My sister can see _____ new kittens.

8. We can ride in _____ truck.

Skills:

Capitalizing the Names of People and Pets

Interviewing

Writing Complete Sentences

Pets Are Family, Too!

Ask two people to tell you the names of their pets. Draw a picture and write a sentence about each person and his or her pet. Use a capital letter to begin the names of people and pets.

Marta has a cat named Cookie.

All in the Family

What does your family like to do together? Write a story about something your family did. Use as many spelling words as you can.

game	name	bake	family
mother	father	brother	sister

_____

_____

_____

_____

_____

_____

_____

_____

✔ Check Your Story

○ I used capital letters for names of people and pets.

○ I used capital letters for names of specific places and things.

TEST YOUR SKILLS — Family Night

My Spelling Test

Find the correct answer. Fill in the circle.

Ask someone to test you on the spelling words.

1. Which sentence has the correct capital letters?
   - ○ My sister and I go to Gus White School.
   - ○ My Brother's cat is named boots.

2. Which sentence uses 's correctly?
   - ○ I helped my brother find his books'.
   - ○ Where are Tim's books?

3. Which word is a noun?
   - ○ game
   - ○ funny

1. _____

2. _____

3. _____

4. _____

5. _____

6. _____

7. _____

8. _____

4. Write the sentence correctly.

   megs brothr and my sisster will play a gam

   _____

   _____

Note: Help your child read the story.

First-Grade Fun

First grade is lots of work! Mrs. Bell is a good teacher. She helps us learn to read, write, and spell. Now I can read a whole book on my own. I can read it to the class. I try to do my best in school. It's fun to spell and write. Mrs. Bell took a look at my work. Then she gave me a sticker. The sticker has a happy face. We work a lot in first grade. But I think first grade is fun!

Find It!

Read the spelling words.
Check off the words you can find in the story.

☑ book	☑ good	☑ look	☑ took
☑ take	☑ read	☑ think	☑ work

How many spelling words did you find? _____

Skills:

Spelling Words with **oo**

Spelling Theme Vocabulary

Visual Memory

Read and Spell	Copy and Spell	Spell It Again!
1. book	_____	_____
2. good	_____	_____
3. look	_____	_____
4. took	_____	_____
5. take	_____	_____
6. read	_____	_____
7. think	_____	_____
8. work	_____	_____

Spelling Time

Skills:

Spelling Words with **oo**

Spelling Theme Vocabulary

Auditory Discrimination

Fill in all the missing letters to make spelling words.

g __ __ d   b __ __ k

r __ __ d   l __ __ k

t __ k __   th __ nk

w __ __ k   t __ __ k

Circle two words in each row that rhyme with the first word.

1.	**book**	hook	lock	cook
2.	**take**	tock	rake	fake
3.	**work**	worm	jerk	perk
4.	**look**	lake	took	crook
5.	**read**	bead	seed	made
6.	**took**	look	make	book
7.	**good**	hood	stood	goat
8.	**think**	sing	sink	blink

Read and Spell

Skills:

Spelling Words with **oo**

Spelling Theme Vocabulary

Visual Memory

Using Sentence Context to Identify Missing Words

Choose the best word to finish each sentence. Write it on the line.

1. Will you _____ this to school?

   take   **think**   **took**

2. It was a _____ book.

   look   **book**   **good**

3. I think you can _____ well.

   read   **good**   **book**

4. _____ for another book to read.

   Took   **Look**   **Book**

5. Do you _____ there is a shark book?

   good   **work**   **think**

6. Find another good _____ to read.

   look   **took**   **book**

Circle the words that are spelled correctly.

1. wurk   work

2. tak   take

3. read   rede

4. theenk   think

A Whole Thought

Skills:

Identifying
Complete
Sentences

A sentence has a whole thought.

> Sentence: **Math is what I like best.**
>
> Not a sentence: **A math game**

If the words make a sentence, color the **YES** star. If the words do <u>not</u> make a sentence, color the **NO** star.

1. A math book

2. Here is my math book

3. I think math is fun

4. In a number

5. Six added to

6. You added three and three

7. Write the number

8. Your math work

Make It a Capital

The names of people, pets, and specific places and things begin with a capital letter.

We go to Big Creek School.

Mr. King is the music teacher.

We sing "America the Beautiful."

Cross out the words that do <u>not</u> need a capital letter.

Teacher	Miss Pool	First Street School
School	Boston	City
Book	Iowa	State
Song	Helper	Mrs. Pine
Mr. Sims	Bus Driver	Curious George

Contractions

A contraction is a short way to write two words.
A contraction uses an apostrophe. (')

you will = you'll

Rewrite each sentence using a contraction.
Use an apostrophe.

1. **Where is** the class?

   _____

2. **We are** at the computers.

   _____

3. **I will** play a word game.

   _____

4. Jessica said **she would** play.

   _____

5. She **did not** win the game.

   _____

didn't   We're   I'll   Where's   she'd

Skills:

Writing
Complete
Sentences

Capitalizing
Names of
Specific Places

My School

Tell about your school. Answer each question with a complete sentence. Use capitals for names of specific places.

1. What is the name of your school?

   _____

   _____

2. On what street is your school?

   _____

   _____

3. In what city or town is your school?

   _____

   _____

4. In what state is your school?

   _____

   _____

5. In what country is your school?

   _____

   _____

Book Magic

Skills:

Writing a
Creative Story

Using Spelling
Words in a
Composition

One day, the teacher opened a book to read to her class. Magic spilled out! The children found themselves in a faraway place. Where did they go? What did they see? How did they get back to school? Write a story. Use your spelling words.

book	good	took	look
take	read	think	work

_____

_____

_____

_____

_____

_____

✓ **Check Your Story**

○   I used complete sentences.

○   I checked my spelling words.

○   I used capitals for specific names and places.

Note: Read the assessment questions to your child.

First-Grade Fun

My Spelling Test

Find the correct answer. Fill in the circle.

1. Which one is a sentence?
   - ○ Your book
   - ○ I like your book

2. Which sentence has the correct capital letters?
   - ○ Our School is in california.
   - ○ Their school is in Texas.

3. Which word is the contraction for **you are**?
   - ○ you'll
   - ○ you're

Ask someone to test you on the spelling words.

1. _____
2. _____
3. _____
4. _____
5. _____
6. _____
7. _____
8. _____

4. Write the sentence correctly.

she didnt werk at lincoln school

_____

_____

Spell & Write • EMC 4537 • © Evan-Moor Corp.

Test Your Skills-Record Form

Unit	Test Page	Topic	Test Your Skills Score (4 possible)	Spelling Test Score (8 possible)
1	12	At the Circus		
2	22	The Playground		
3	32	Fourth of July		
4	42	Story of the Year		
5	52	Good Morning!		
6	62	Sing a Song		
7	72	Be Safe		
8	82	Away We Go!		
9	92	On the Farm		
10	102	Pet Show		
11	112	Family Night		
12	122	First-Grade Fun		

Pull-out Spelling Lists

Use these lists to give spelling tests, post on the refrigerator, and for extra practice.

Unit 1 At the Circus	Unit 2 The Playground	Unit 3 Fourth of July
1. can	1. up	1. hat
2. pan	2. us	2. hot
3. man	3. run	3. hand
4. cat	4. fun	4. sand
5. sat	5. jump	5. red
6. wish	6. to	6. blue
7. like	7. ship	7. white
8. lady	8. game	8. flag

Pull-out Spelling Lists

Use these lists to give spelling tests, post on the refrigerator, and for extra practice.

Unit 4 Story of the Year	Unit 5 Good Morning!	Unit 6 Sing a Song
1. make	1. we	1. so
2. shake	2. me	2. no
3. lake	3. tree	3. note
4. rake	4. see	4. home
5. sun	5. hear	5. do
6. snow	6. hold	6. you
7. grow	7. smell	7. nice
8. after	8. eat	8. sing

Pull-out Spelling Lists

Use these lists to give spelling tests, post on the refrigerator, and for extra practice.

Unit 7 Be Safe	Unit 8 Away We Go!	Unit 9 On the Farm
1. day	1. car	1. cow
2. may	2. far	2. now
3. stay	3. start	3. down
4. play	4. are	4. town
5. stop	5. go	5. brown
6. look	6. ride	6. farm
7. rule	7. fly	7. barn
8. safe	8. with	8. help

Pull-out Spelling Lists

Use these lists to give spelling tests, post on the refrigerator, and for extra practice.

Unit 10 Pet Show	Unit 11 Family Night	Unit 12 First-Grade Fun
1. funny	1. game	1. book
2. bunny	2. name	2. good
3. puppy	3. bake	3. look
4. happy	4. family	4. took
5. little	5. mother	5. take
6. kitten	6. father	6. read
7. pet	7. sister	7. think
8. my	8. brother	8. work

Answer Key

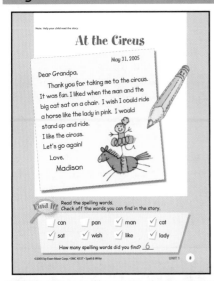

At the Circus

May 31, 2005

Dear Grandpa,

Thank you for taking me to the circus. It was fun. I liked when the man and the big cat sat on a chair. I wish I could ride a horse like the lady in pink. I would stand up and ride.

I like the circus.

Let's go again!

Love,

Madison

Find it! Read the spelling words. Check off the words you can find in the story.

☐ can ☐ pan ✓ man ✓ cat
✓ sat ✓ wish ✓ like ✓ lady

How many spelling words did you find? 6

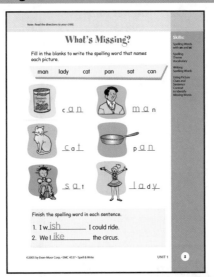

What's Missing?

Fill in the blanks to write the spelling word that names each picture.

| man | lady | cat | pan | sat | can |

c a n   m a n

c a t   p a n

s a t   l a d y

Finish the spelling word in each sentence.

1. I w ish I could ride.
2. I l ike the circus.

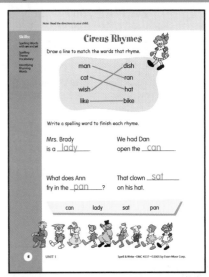

Circus Rhymes

Draw a line to match the words that rhyme.

man — dish
cat — ran
wish — hat
like — bike

Write a spelling word to finish each rhyme.

Mrs. Brady is a lady

We had Dan open the can

What does Ann fry in the pan ?

That clown sat on his hat.

| can | lady | sat | pan |

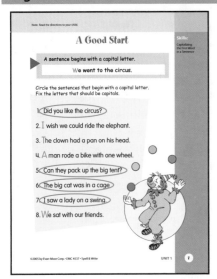

A Good Start

A sentence begins with a capital letter.

We went to the circus.

Circle the sentences that begin with a capital letter. Fix the letters that should be capitals.

1. (Did you like the circus?)
2. I wish we could ride the elephant.
3. The clown had a pan on his head.
4. A man rode a bike with one wheel.
5. (Can they pack up the big tent?)
6. (The big cat was in a cage)
7. (I saw a lady on a swing)
8. We sat with our friends.

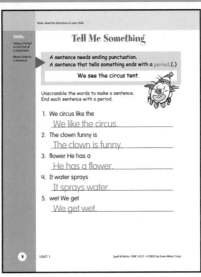

Tell Me Something

A sentence needs ending punctuation.
A sentence that tells something ends with a period. (.)

We see the circus tent.

Unscramble the words to make a sentence. End each sentence with a period.

1. We circus like the
   We like the circus.
2. The clown funny is
   The clown is funny.
3. flower He has a
   He has a flower.
4. It water sprays
   It sprays water.
5. wet We get
   We get wet.

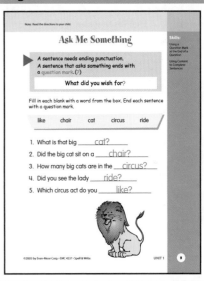

Ask Me Something

A sentence needs ending punctuation.
A sentence that asks something ends with a question mark. (?)

What did you wish for?

Fill in each blank with a word from the box. End each sentence with a question mark.

| like | chair | cat | circus | ride |

1. What is that big cat?
2. Did the big cat sit on a chair?
3. How many big cats are in the circus?
4. Did you see the lady ride?
5. Which circus act do you like?

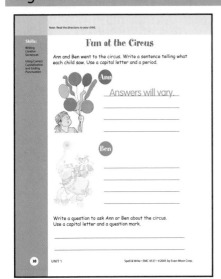

Fun at the Circus

Ann and Ben went to the circus. Write a sentence telling what each child saw. Use a capital letter and a period.

Ann

Answers will vary.

Ben

Write a question to ask Ann or Ben about the circus. Use a capital letter and a question mark.

The Big Show

Finish the story. Use as many spelling words as you can.

| can | pan | man | cat |
| sat | wish | like | lady |

Ann and Ben played circus. They made a tent in the yard. Answers will vary.

✓ Check Your Story

○ I used a capital letter to begin each sentence.
○ I used a period or question mark at the end of each sentence.

TEST YOUR SKILLS At the Circus

My Spelling Test

Find the correct answer. Fill in the circle.

Ask someone to test you on the spelling words.

1. Which punctuation mark goes at the end of the sentence?
   We like the circus__
   ● period (.)
   ○ question mark (?)

2. Which punctuation mark goes at the end of the sentence?
   Did you see the big cat__
   ○ period (.)
   ● question mark (?)

3. Which sentence has the correct capital letter?
   ○ here is the circus Tent.
   ● Where is your ticket?

1. _____
2. _____
3. _____
4. _____
5. _____
6. _____
7. _____
8. _____

4. Write the sentence correctly.
   did you wich for a kat
   Did you wish for a cat?

Page 13

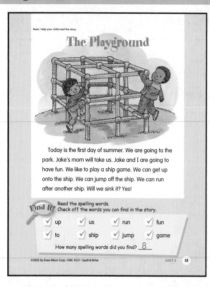

Note: Help your child read the story.

The Playground

Today is the first day of summer. We are going to the park. Jake's mom will take us. Jake and I are going to have fun. We like to play a ship game. We can get up onto the ship. We can jump off the ship. We can run after another ship. Will we sink it? Yes!

Find It! Read the spelling words. Check off the words you can find in the story.

✓ up   ✓ us   ✓ run   ✓ fun
✓ to   ✓ ship   ✓ jump   ✓ game

How many spelling words did you find? 8

Page 15

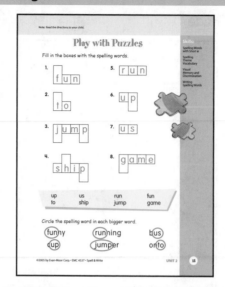

Note: Read the directions to your child.

Play with Puzzles

Fill in the boxes with the spelling words.

1. f u n
2. t o
3. j u m p
4. s h i p
5. r u n
6. u p
7. u s
8. g a m e

up   us   run   fun
to   ship   jump   game

Circle the spelling word in each bigger word.

funny   running   bus
cup   jumper   onto

Skills:
Spelling Words with Short u
Spelling Theme Vocabulary
Visual Memory and Discrimination
Writing Spelling Words

Page 16

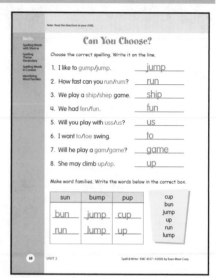

Note: Read the directions to your child.

Skills:
Spelling Words with Short u
Spelling Theme Vocabulary
Spelling Words in Context
Identifying Word Families

Can You Choose?

Choose the correct spelling. Write it on the line.

1. I like to gump/jump. jump
2. How fast can you run/rum? run
3. We play a ship/shep game. ship
4. We had fen/fun. fun
5. Will you play with uss/us? us
6. I want to/toe swing. to
7. Will he play a gam/game? game
8. She may climb up/op. up

Make word families. Write the words below in the correct box.

sun	bump	pup
bun	jump	cup
run	lump	up

cup
bun
jump
up
run
lump

Page 17

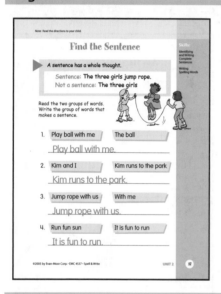

Note: Read the directions to your child.

Find the Sentence

A sentence has a whole thought.

Sentence: The three girls jump rope.
Not a sentence: The three girls

Read the two groups of words. Write the group of words that makes a sentence.

1. Play ball with me   The ball
   Play ball with me.
2. Kim and I   Kim runs to the park
   Kim runs to the park.
3. Jump rope with us   With me
   Jump rope with us.
4. Run fun sun   It is fun to run
   It is fun to run.

Skills:
Identifying and Writing Complete Sentences
Writing Spelling Words

Page 18

Note: Read the directions to your child.

Skills:
Capitalizing the First Word in a Sentence

Use a Capital

A sentence begins with a capital letter.

Dogs play in the park.

Does the sentence begin with a capital letter? Circle yes or no.

1. We run in the park.   yes   no
2. go up the slide.   yes   no
3. we have fun in the jump house.   yes   no
4. Let's play a game.   yes   no
5. I have a ball.   yes   no

Write a sentence that goes with each picture. Use a capital letter to begin each sentence.

Answers will vary.

Page 19

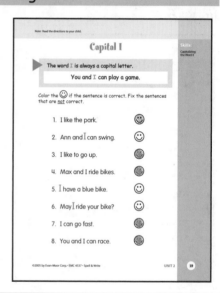

Note: Read the directions to your child.

Capital I

The word I is always a capital letter.

You and I can play a game.

Color the ☺ if the sentence is correct. Fix the sentences that are not correct.

1. I like the park.   ☺
2. Ann and I can swing.   ☺
3. I like to go up.   ☺
4. Max and I ride bikes.   ☺
5. I have a blue bike.   ☺
6. May I ride your bike?   ☺
7. I can go fast.   ☺
8. You and I can race.   ☺

Skills:
Capitalizing the Word I

Page 20

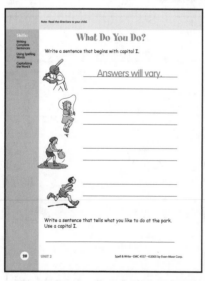

Note: Read the directions to your child.

Skills:
Writing Complete Sentences
Using Spelling Words
Capitalizing the Word I

What Do You Do?

Write a sentence that begins with capital I.

Answers will vary.

Write a sentence that tells what you like to do at the park. Use a capital I.

Page 21

Note: Read the directions to your child.

Friends Have Fun

Finish the story.

My friend's name is Answers will vary.
We like to play _____
We also like to _____
_____
My friend and _____ have fun.

Draw a picture of yourself and your friend playing. Write a sentence that tells about your picture.

My friend and _____ are _____

Skills:
Writing a Creative Story
Completing Sentences
Using Capital I

Page 22

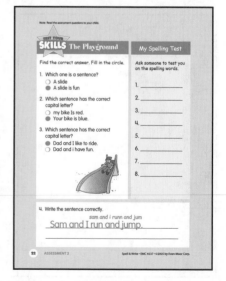

Note: Read the assessment questions to your child.

TEST YOUR SKILLS The Playground

Find the correct answer. Fill in the circle.

1. Which one is a sentence?
   ○ A slide
   ● A slide is fun
2. Which sentence has the correct capital letter?
   ○ my bike Is red.
   ● Your bike is blue.
3. Which sentence has the correct capital letter?
   ● Dad and I like to ride.
   ○ Dad and i have fun.

4. Write the sentence correctly.
   sam and i runn and jum
   Sam and I run and jump.

My Spelling Test

Ask someone to test you on the spelling words.

1. _____
2. _____
3. _____
4. _____
5. _____
6. _____
7. _____
8. _____

Page 23

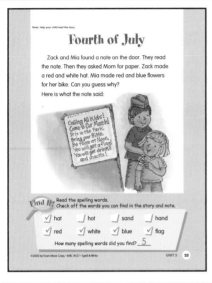

Fourth of July

Zack and Mia found a note on the door. They read the note. Then they asked Mom for paper. Zack made a red and white hat. Mia made red and blue flowers for her bike. Can you guess why?
Here is what the note said:

Calling All Kids! Come to Our Party! It is in the Park. Bring your Bike. Be there at Noon. You will get a flag! You will get drinks and snacks!

Find it! Read the spelling words. Check off the words you can find in the story and note.

✓ hat ☐ hot ☐ sand ☐ hand
✓ red ✓ white ✓ blue ✓ flag

How many spelling words did you find? 5

Page 25

Spell It

Mark an X on the misspelled words. Spell them correctly on the lines.

1. What color is the flage? — flag
2. This box is red, whit, and blue. — white
3. The sun is hout. — hot
4. Put on your blue het. — hat
5. Play in the sad with me. — sand

Circle each correct spelling.

1. hamd — (hand) — (hand) — hande
2. (white) — wite — wite — (white)
3. bue — bloo — (blue) — (blue)
4. hawt — haht — (hot) — howt

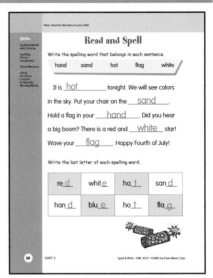

Page 26

Read and Spell

Write the spelling word that belongs in each sentence.

| hand | sand | hot | flag | white |

It is __hot__ tonight. We will see colors in the sky. Put your chair on the __sand__.
Hold a flag in your __hand__. Did you hear a big boom? There is a red and __white__ star!
Wave your __flag__. Happy Fourth of July!

Write the last letter of each spelling word.

| re_d_ | whit_e_ | ha_t_ | san_d_ |
| han_d_ | blu_e_ | ho_t_ | fla_g_ |

Page 27

Is It a Sentence?

▶ A sentence has a whole thought.
Sentence: Where is my red hat?
Not a sentence: My red hat

If the words make a sentence, color the YES star. If the words do **not** make a sentence, color the NO star.

1. Your hat is nice — YES
2. Blue hat — NO
3. The flag is blue and white — YES
4. Dad put the chair on the sand — YES
5. Red, white, and blue — NO
6. The sand is hot — YES
7. Hand sand band land — NO
8. Please hand me a hot dog — YES

Page 28

Capital Letters

▶ A sentence begins with a capital letter.
We saw the band march.

Circle the sentences that begin with a capital letter. Fix the letters that should be capitals.

1. Do you know what today is?
2. Today is a holiday.
3. (Our country has a birthday.)
4. Fly your flag.
5. Wear red, white, and blue.
6. Wear a hat in the hot sun.
7. (We can hear the band play.)
8. My brother plays a big drum.

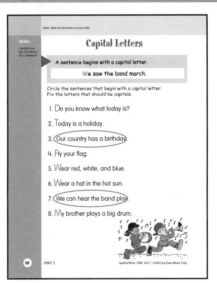

Page 29

Asking or Telling?

▶ A sentence needs ending punctuation.
A sentence that tells something ends with a period. (.)
The band plays music.
A sentence that asks something ends with a question mark. (?)
What songs do they play?

Read each sentence. Draw a line to show if it is an asking sentence or a telling sentence. The first one has been done for you.

Do you play in a band? — Asking Sentence
I like to march.
We all have red hats.
Where is your hat?
Can you carry the flag? — Telling Sentence
Here is the flag.
Can you wave your flag?

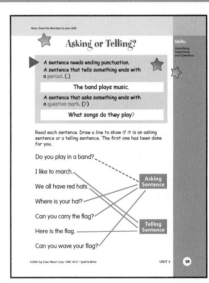

Page 30

Fun on the Fourth

Sam and Lisa had fun on the Fourth of July. Write a sentence telling what each child did. Use a capital letter and a period.

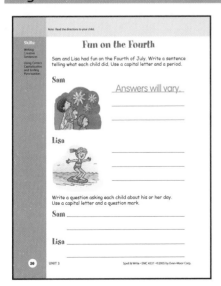

Sam — Answers will vary.

Lisa

Write a question asking each child about his or her day. Use a capital letter and a question mark.

Sam

Lisa

Page 31

Holiday Fun

What do you like to do on the Fourth of July? Write about it. Use as many spelling words as you can.

| hat | hot | hand | sand |
| red | blue | white | flag |

Answers will vary.

✓ **Check Your Story**
○ I used a capital letter to begin each sentence.
○ I used a period or question mark at the end of each sentence.

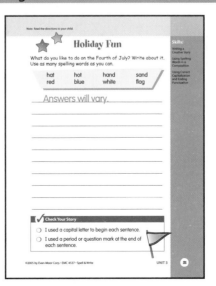

Page 32

TEST YOUR SKILLS — Fourth of July

Find the correct answer. Fill in the circle.

1. Which punctuation mark goes at the end of the sentence?
Did you march with the band___
○ period (.)
● question mark (?)

2. Which one is a sentence?
○ The white sand
● The sand is hot

3. Which sentence has the correct capital letter?
● This hat is too big for me.
○ my Red hat is just right.

4. Write the sentence correctly.
my flag is rad, white, and blu
__My flag is red, white, and blue.__

My Spelling Test

Ask someone to test you on the spelling words.

1. _____
2. _____
3. _____
4. _____
5. _____
6. _____
7. _____
8. _____

Page 33

Note: Help your child read the story.

Story of the Year

The story of the year goes like this:

In the **spring**, baby birds and lambs are born. The days get warmer. Little plants begin to grow.

Summer brings long days of hot sun. The garden is full of flowers and bees. We go to the beach.

In the **fall**, leaves turn yellow, red, and brown. They fall from the trees. We rake them up.

Winter comes and brings the cold. A bear sleeps. The lake has a cover of ice. We have fun in the snow. We make tracks.

Year after year, the story goes on. First spring comes, then summer, fall, and winter.

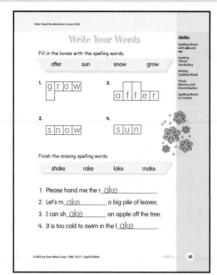

Find It! Read the spelling words. Check off the words you can find in the story.

- ✓ make
- ☐ shake
- ✓ lake
- ✓ rake
- ✓ sun
- ✓ snow
- ✓ grow
- ☐ after

How many spelling words did you find? __7__

©2005 by Evan-Moor Corp. • EMC 4537 • Spell & Write   UNIT 4   33

Page 35

Note: Read the directions to your child.

Write Your Words

Fill in the boxes with the spelling words.

after   sun   snow   grow

1. g r o w
3. a f t e r
2. s n o w
4. s u n

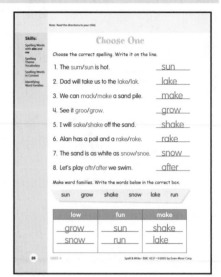

Finish the missing spelling words.

shake   rake   lake   make

1. Please hand me the r _ake_
2. Let's m _ake_ a big pile of leaves.
3. I can sh _ake_ an apple off the tree.
4. It is too cold to swim in the l _ake_.

©2005 by Evan-Moor Corp. • EMC 4537 • Spell & Write   UNIT 4   35

Skills:
Spelling Words with **ake** and **ow**
Spelling Theme Vocabulary
Writing Memory and Discrimination
Visual Memory and Discrimination
Spelling Words in Context

Page 36

Note: Read the directions to your child.

Skills:
Spelling Words with **ake** and **ow**
Spelling Theme Vocabulary
Spelling Words in Context
Identifying Word Families

Choose One

Choose the correct spelling. Write it on the line.

1. The sum/sun is hot. __sun__
2. Dad will take us to the lake/lak. __lake__
3. We can mack/make a sand pile. __make__
4. See it groo/grow. __grow__
5. I will sake/shake off the sand. __shake__
6. Alan has a pail and a rake/roke. __rake__
7. The sand is as white as snow/snoe. __snow__
8. Let's play aftr/after we swim. __after__

Make word families. Write the words below in the correct box.

sun   grow   shake   snow   lake   run

low	fun	make
grow	sun	shake
snow	run	lake

36   UNIT 4   Spell & Write • EMC 4537 • ©2005 by Evan-Moor Corp.

Page 37

Note: Read the directions to your child.

Nouns Name Things

Skills:
Identifying Nouns

Some words name things. These words are called nouns.

The lady has a blue hat.

Color each apple that names something.

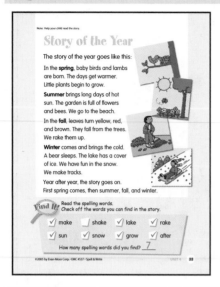

©2005 by Evan-Moor Corp. • EMC 4537 • Spell & Write   UNIT 4   37

Page 38

Note: Read the directions to your child.

Skills:
Using 's to Show Possession

Summer Fun

When something belongs to one person, add 's to the name of the person.

We swim in Amy's pool.

Draw a line to show to whom each thing belongs.

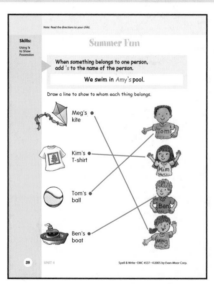

Meg's kite
Kim's T-shirt
Tom's ball
Ben's boat

38   UNIT 4   Spell & Write • EMC 4537 • ©2005 by Evan-Moor Corp.

Page 39

Note: Read the directions to your child.

Winter Fun

Skills:
Using 's to Show Possession

Write the name to show who owns each thing. Use 's.

1. Matt has skates. __Matt's__ skates	2. Jan has boots. __Jan's__ boots
3. Dan has a hat. __Dan's__ hat	4. Maria has mittens. __Maria's__ mittens
5. Ana has a sled. __Ana's__ sled	6. Marco has a scarf. __Marco's__ scarf

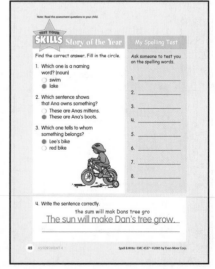

©2005 by Evan-Moor Corp. • EMC 4537 • Spell & Write   UNIT 4   39

Page 40

Note: Read the directions to your child.

Skills:
Writing Creative Sentences
Identifying Nouns

Around the Year

Finish each sentence to tell about the season. Circle the nouns in your sentences.

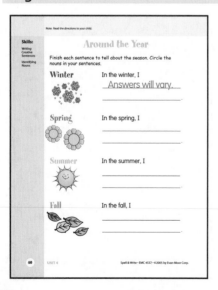

Winter   In the winter, I __Answers will vary.__

Spring   In the spring, I

Summer   In the summer, I

Fall   In the fall, I

40   UNIT 4   Spell & Write • EMC 4537 • ©2005 by Evan-Moor Corp.

Page 41

Note: Read the directions to your child.

Time of Year

Skills:
Writing a Poem
Using 's to Show Possession

Finish the poem. Fill in the name of the season.

winter   spring   fall   summer

I like spring.
  I like __spring__ 's rain.
  I like __spring__ 's soft, quiet rain.

I like summer.
  I like __summer__ 's sun.
  I like __summer__ 's hot, hot sun.

I like fall.
  I like __fall__ 's colors.
  I like __fall__ 's red and yellow leaves.

I like winter.
  I like __winter__ 's snow.
  I like __winter__ 's white, white snow.

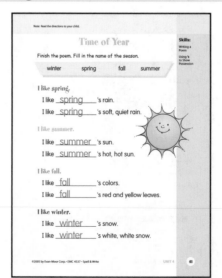

©2005 by Evan-Moor Corp. • EMC 4537 • Spell & Write   UNIT 4   41

Page 42

Note: Read the assessment questions to your child.

TEST YOUR SKILLS Story of the Year

Find the correct answer. Fill in the circle.

1. Which one is a naming word? (noun)
   ○ swim
   ● lake

2. Which sentence shows that Ana owns something?
   ○ These are Anas mittens.
   ● These are Ana's boots.

3. Which one tells to whom something belongs?
   ● Lee's bike
   ○ red bike

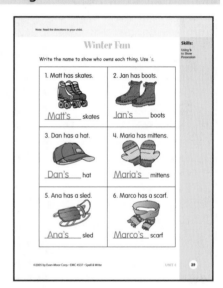

4. Write the sentence correctly.
   the sum will mak Dans tree gro
   __The sun will make Dan's tree grow.__

My Spelling Test

Ask someone to test you on the spelling words.

1. _____
2. _____
3. _____
4. _____
5. _____
6. _____
7. _____
8. _____

42   ASSESSMENT 4   Spell & Write • EMC 4537 • ©2005 by Evan-Moor Corp.

136   Spell & Write • EMC 4537 • © Evan-Moor Corp.

Good Morning!

Wake up! It's morning. What do you see?
  The sun in the sky
  And birds in a tree.

Wake up! It's morning. What do you hear?
  Someone is singing
  A song soft and clear.

Wake up! It's morning. What do you hold?
  The covers around me
  To keep out the cold.

Wake up! It's morning. What do you smell?
  Someone is frying
  An egg, I can tell.

Wake up! It's morning. What do you eat?
  Warm oats and cold milk,
  And berries so sweet.

Find It! Read the spelling words. Check off the words you can find in the story.
✓ we ✓ me ✓ tree ✓ see
✓ hear ✓ hold ✓ smell ✓ eat
How many spelling words did you find? 7

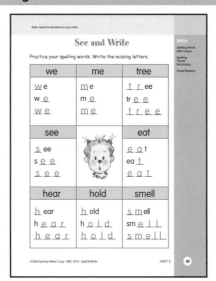

See and Write

Practice your spelling words. Write the missing letters.

we	me	tree
w e	m e	t r ee
w e	m e	tr ee
w e	m e	t r ee
see		eat
s ee		e a t
s ee		ea t
s ee		e a t
hear	hold	smell
h ear	h old	s m ell
h ear	h old	sm ell
h ear	h old	smell

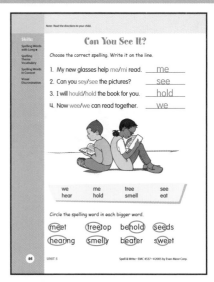

Can You See It?

Choose the correct spelling. Write it on the line.

1. My new glasses help me/mi read. _____ me
2. Can you sey/see the pictures? _____ see
3. I will hould/hold the book for you. _____ hold
4. Now wee/we can read together. _____ we

| we | me | tree | see |
| hear | hold | smell | eat |

Circle the spelling word in each bigger word.
(meet) (treetop) behold (seeds)
(hearing) (smelly) beater sweet

Find the Verbs

Some words tell what is happening. These words are called verbs.

We smell the popcorn.
(What is happening)

Color the verbs.
[hear] [eat] [hold]
egg
[smell] we
tree [see]

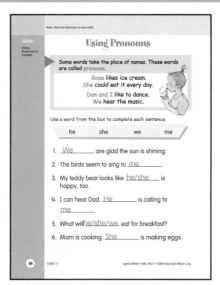

Using Pronouns

Some words take the place of names. These words are called pronouns.

Rose likes ice cream.
She could eat it every day.
Dan and I like to dance.
We hear the music.

Use a word from the box to complete each sentence.

| he | she | we | me |

1. We are glad the sun is shining.
2. The birds seem to sing to me.
3. My teddy bear looks like he/she is happy, too.
4. I can hear Dad. He is calling to me.
5. What will he/she/we eat for breakfast?
6. Mom is cooking. She is making eggs.

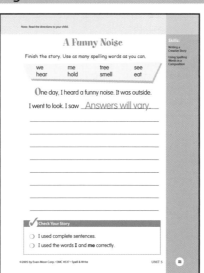

I or Me?

Use I when you are the person doing something.
I bake cookies with Mother.
Use me when something happens to you.
Mother gave me a cookie.

Fill in the blanks with I or me.

1. I have fun cooking.
2. Father and I make cookies.
3. He lets me help.
4. I put in flour and sugar.
5. Father helps me mix the batter.
6. I put the cookies on a plate.
7. Father gives me a taste.
8. I think they are good.

Using My Senses

Write a sentence about something you like to see, hear, touch, smell, and taste. Use I in your sentences.

see — Answers will vary.
hear
touch
smell
taste

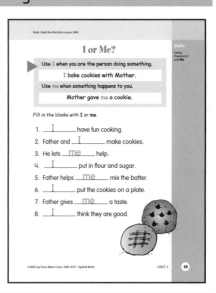

A Funny Noise

Finish the story. Use as many spelling words as you can.

| we | me | tree | see |
| hear | hold | smell | eat |

One day, I heard a funny noise. It was outside.
I went to look. I saw Answers will vary.

✓ Check Your Story
○ I used complete sentences.
○ I used the words I and me correctly.

TEST YOUR **SKILLS** Good Morning!   My Spelling Test

Find the correct answer. Fill in the circle.

1. Which word tells what is happening?
  ● eat
  ○ tree
2. Which pronoun goes in the blank?
  Sam gave _____ his book.
  ○ I
  ● me
3. Which pronoun goes in the blank?
  Jenny can smell the flower.
  _____ likes flowers.
  ○ We
  ● She

4. Write the sentence correctly.
  wee sea an apple on the tre
  We see an apple on the tree.

Ask someone to test you on the spelling words.
1. _____
2. _____
3. _____
4. _____
5. _____
6. _____
7. _____
8. _____

Page 53 — Sing a Song

Note: Help your child read the story.

Sing a Song

A song needs notes.
Hum a song you know.
Can you hear the notes
go up and down?

A song needs a beat.
You can clap the beat
of a song. Clap
one—two—three—four!

Some songs have
words. The words may
be **happy**, **silly**, **sad**,
or **nice**. Words help
you feel the song.

So sing your song the
way you feel it!

Find It! Read the spelling words.
Check off the words you can find in the story.

- ✓ so
- ☐ no
- ✓ note
- ☐ home
- ☐ do
- ✓ you
- ✓ nice
- ✓ sing

How many spelling words did you find? __5__

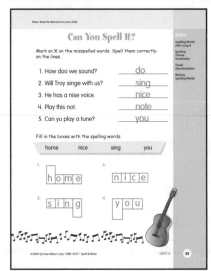

Page 55 — Can You Spell It?

Note: Read the directions to your child.

Can You Spell It?

Skills: Spelling Words with Long e • Spelling Theme Vocabulary • Visual Discrimination • Writing Spelling Words

Mark an X on the misspelled words. Spell them correctly
on the lines.

1. How doo we sound? __do__
2. Will Troy singe with us? __sing__
3. He has a nise voice. __nice__
4. Play this not. __note__
5. Can yu play a tune? __you__

Fill in the boxes with the spelling words.

| home | nice | sing | you |

1. h o m e
2. s i n g
3. n i c e
4. y o u

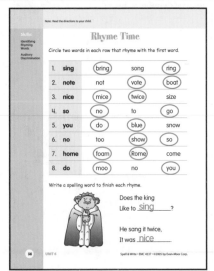

Page 56 — Rhyme Time

Note: Read the directions to your child.

Skills: Identifying Rhyming Words • Auditory Discrimination

Rhyme Time

Circle two words in each row that rhyme with the first word.

1.	sing	(bring)	song	(ring)
2.	note	not	(vote)	(boat)
3.	nice	(mice)	(twice)	size
4.	so	no	to	(go)
5.	you	(do)	(blue)	snow
6.	no	too	(show)	(so)
7.	home	(foam)	(Rome)	come
8.	do	(moo)	no	(you)

Write a spelling word to finish each rhyme.

Does the king
Like to __sing__?

He sang it twice,
It was __nice__

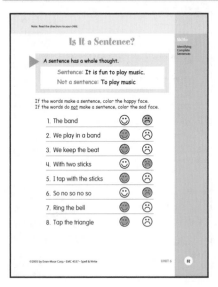

Page 57 — Is It a Sentence?

Note: Read the directions to your child.

Skills: Identifying Complete Sentences

Is It a Sentence?

A sentence has a whole thought.

Sentence: **It is fun to play music.**
Not a sentence: **To play music**

If the words make a sentence, color the happy face.
If the words do _not_ make a sentence, color the sad face.

1. The band ☺ ☹
2. We play in a band ☺ ☹
3. We keep the beat ☺ ☹
4. With two sticks ☺ ☹
5. I tap with the sticks ☺ ☹
6. So no so no so ☺ ☹
7. Ring the bell ☺ ☹
8. Tap the triangle ☺ ☹

Page 58 — Looking for I

Note: Read the directions to your child.

Skills: Using Capital I

Looking for I

Circle the sentences that have a capital I.
Fix the sentences that do _not_ have a capital I.

1. (Rita and I have fun)
2. I turn on the radio.
3. (I like to sing and dance)
4. When the music plays, I listen.
5. (I show Rita the steps)
6. She and I practice at home.
7. I can snap my fingers.
8. (Rita and I can teach you, too)

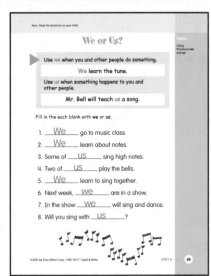

Page 59 — We or Us?

Note: Read the directions to your child.

Skills: Using Pronouns we and us

We or Us?

Use **we** when you and other people do something.

We learn the tune.

Use **us** when something happens to you and
other people.

Mr. Bell will teach **us** a song.

Fill in the each blank with we or us.

1. __We__ go to music class.
2. __We__ learn about notes.
3. Some of __us__ sing high notes.
4. Two of __us__ play the bells.
5. __We__ learn to sing together.
6. Next week, __we__ are in a show.
7. In the show __we__ will sing and dance.
8. Will you sing with __us__?

Page 60 — My Music

Note: Read the directions to your child.

Skills: Using Capital I

My Music

Do you play or sing music? What would you like to play?
What would you like to sing? Write about it. Use some of
your spelling words.

__Answers will vary.__

Draw a picture of yourself making music.

✓ Check Your Story
- ☐ I used complete sentences.
- ☐ I used capital I correctly.

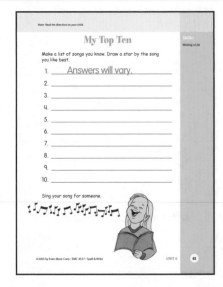

Page 61 — My Top Ten

Note: Read the directions to your child.

Skills: Writing a List

My Top Ten

Make a list of songs you know. Draw a star by the song
you like best.

1. __Answers will vary.__
2. _____
3. _____
4. _____
5. _____
6. _____
7. _____
8. _____
9. _____
10. _____

Sing your song for someone.

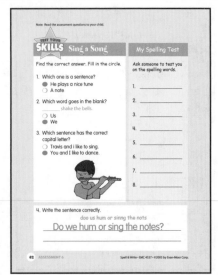

Page 62 — Sing a Song

Note: Read the assessment questions to your child.

TEST YOUR SKILLS — Sing a Song

Find the correct answer. Fill in the circle.

1. Which one is a sentence?
   - ● He plays a nice tune
   - ○ A note
2. Which word goes in the blank?
   ____ shake the bells.
   - ○ Us
   - ● We
3. Which sentence has the correct
   capital letter?
   - ○ Travis and i like to sing.
   - ● You and I like to dance.

My Spelling Test

Ask someone to test you
on the spelling words.

1. _____
2. _____
3. _____
4. _____
5. _____
6. _____
7. _____
8. _____

4. Write the sentence correctly.
   doo us hum or sing the nots
   __Do we hum or sing the notes?__

Spell & Write • EMC 4537 • © Evan-Moor Corp.

Page 63

Note: Help your child read the story.

Be Safe

At school, Min and Adam learned how to be safe. A firefighter came to visit. He showed the children his gear and his truck. He told them how to stay safe. He gave them a list. It has a good rule to remember. If you see a fire, dial 9-1-1. Min and Adam like to play with toy fire trucks. They may want to fight fires one day.

Find It! Read the spelling words. Check off the words you can find in the story.

- ✓ day
- ✓ may
- ✓ stay
- ✓ play
- ☐ stop
- ☐ look
- ✓ rule
- ✓ safe

How many spelling words did you find? **6**

©2005 by Evan-Moor Corp. • EMC 4537 • Spell & Write   UNIT 7   63

Page 65

Note: Read the directions to your child.

Write Your Words

Skills: Spelling Words with **ay** / Writing Spelling Words / Visual Memory and Discrimination

Fill in the boxes with the spelling words.

| day | may | stay | play |

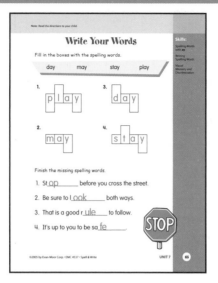

1. p l a y
3. d a y
2. m a y
4. s t a y

Finish the missing spelling words.

1. St **op** before you cross the street.
2. Be sure to l **ook** both ways.
3. That is a good r **ule** to follow.
4. It's up to you to be sa **fe** .

©2005 by Evan-Moor Corp. • EMC 4537 • Spell & Write   UNIT 7   65

Page 66

Note: Read the directions to your child.

Skills: Using Sentence Context to Identify Missing Words / Writing Spelling Words / Using Vowel Sounds

Play It Safe

Fill in the missing words.

| may | stay | day | play |

1. Will you **stay** and play?
2. Do not **play** in the street.
3. You **may** get hurt.
4. Have a safe **day** .

Write letters in the blanks to make spelling words.

| oo | u | o | ay | a |

d **ay**	m **ay**
st **o** p	r **u** le
s **a** fe	st **ay**
l **oo** k	pl **ay**

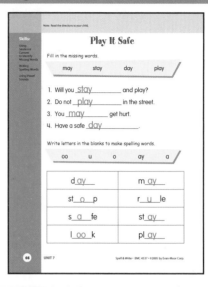

66   UNIT 7   Spell & Write • EMC 4537 • ©2005 by Evan-Moor Corp.

Page 67

Note: Read the directions to your child.

What Happened?

Skills: Identifying and Writing Verbs / Using Sentence Context to Identify Missing Words

> Some words tell what is happening or what already happened. These words are called verbs.
>
> We see the red light.
> (What is happening)
> We waited to cross the street.
> (What already happened)

Fill in the blanks with words from the box. Circle the words that tell what happened.

| do | stay | look | stop |
| play | fell | called | came |

1. We try to **stay** safe.
2. We know what to **do** .
3. We do not **play** in the street.
4. We **stop** at every corner.
5. We always **look** both ways.
6. One time, I **fell** down in the street.
7. I **called** to my friend for help.
8. She **came** right away.

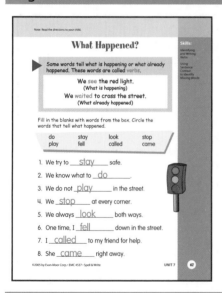

©2005 by Evan-Moor Corp. • EMC 4537 • Spell & Write   UNIT 7   67

Page 68

Note: Read the directions to your child.

Skills: Using Verbs is and are / Using Sentence Context to Identify Missing Words

Bike Safety

> Use is with one and are with more than one.
> That is a nice bike.
> Our bikes are the same color.

Fill in each blank with is or are.

1. Here **is** my new bike.
2. There **are** three bikes in our family.
3. What **is** the bike rule?
4. It **is** good to look for cars.
5. Two kids **are** at the stop sign.
6. This **is** a helmet.
7. It **is** safe to wear a helmet when you ride.
8. Our helmets **are** purple.

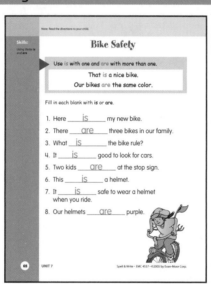

68   UNIT 7   Spell & Write • EMC 4537 • ©2005 by Evan-Moor Corp.

Page 69

Note: Read the directions to your child.

Important to Know

Skills: Using Pronouns they and them

> Use they when several people do something.
> Use them when something happens to several people.
> They got lost in the store.
> Mother couldn't find them.

Fill in each blank with they or them.

1. **They** asked the guard for help.
2. The guard helped **them** .
3. What did **they** tell the guard?
4. **They** knew their mother's name.
5. Mother was so happy to see **them** .
6. Do **they** know their phone number?
7. Tell **them** to learn their address.

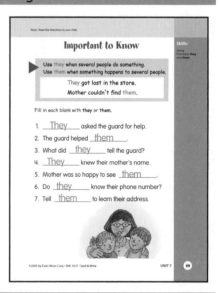

©2005 by Evan-Moor Corp. • EMC 4537 • Spell & Write   UNIT 7   69

Page 70

Note: Read the directions to your child.

Skills: Writing Complete Sentences / Using Picture Clues / Identifying Verbs

Keep Safe

Tell how each child is being safe.

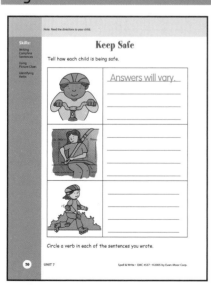

Answers will vary.

Circle a verb in each of the sentences you wrote.

70   UNIT 7   Spell & Write • EMC 4537 • ©2005 by Evan-Moor Corp.

Page 71

Note: Read the directions to your child.

School Rules

Skills: Writing a Creative Story / Using Spelling Words in a Composition

Read the safety rule. Write a story about a boy who didn't follow the rule. How many spelling words can you use in your story?

Rule: Walk, don't run in school.

| day | stop | may | look |
| stay | rule | play | safe |

Answers will vary.

✓ Check Your Story
- ○ I used complete sentences.
- ○ I used capital letters correctly.
- ○ I used punctuation marks.

©2005 by Evan-Moor Corp. • EMC 4537 • Spell & Write   UNIT 7   71

Page 72

Note: Read the assessment questions to your child.

TEST YOUR SKILLS Be Safe

Find the correct answer. Fill in the circle.

1. Which word tells what is happening? (verb)
   - ● look
   - ○ them
2. Which word goes in the blank?
   The fire _____ out.
   - ● is
   - ○ are
3. Which word goes in the blank?
   Did _____ stop at the stop sign?
   - ○ them
   - ● they

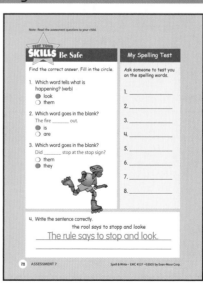

4. Write the sentence correctly.
   the rool says to stopp and looke
   The rule says to stop and look.

| My Spelling Test |
| Ask someone to test you on the spelling words. |
| 1. _____ |
| 2. _____ |
| 3. _____ |
| 4. _____ |
| 5. _____ |
| 6. _____ |
| 7. _____ |
| 8. _____ |

72   ASSESSMENT 7   Spell & Write • EMC 4537 • ©2005 by Evan-Moor Corp.

Page 73

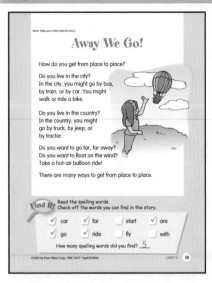

Page 75

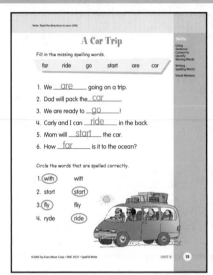

Page 76

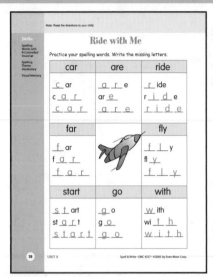

Page 77

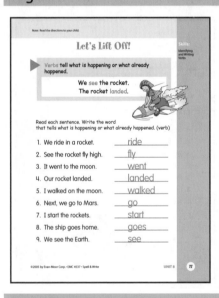

Page 78

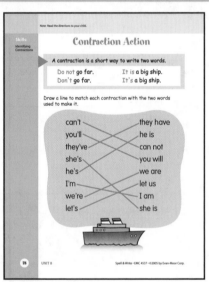

Page 79

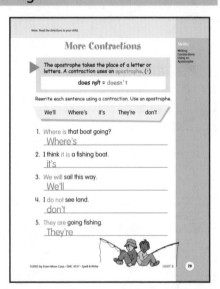

Page 80

Page 81

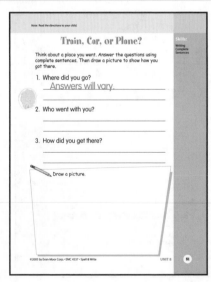

Page 82

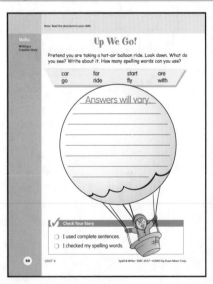

On the Farm

The rooster crows, "Cock-a-doodle-do!" It's time for the farm animals to wake up. It's time for the farmer to wake up, too. The farmer eats fresh eggs for breakfast. Now it is time to walk down to the barn. Twinkle, the brown cow, waits for him. She knows it's milking time. The cats that live in the barn want to help. They want some of Twinkle's fresh milk, too!

Find It! Read the spelling words.
Check off the words you can find in the story.

✓ cow ✓ now ✓ down ☐ town
✓ brown ✓ farm ✓ barn ✓ help

How many spelling words did you find? 7

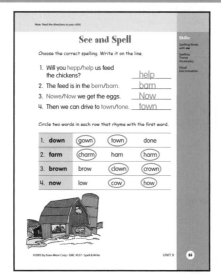

See and Spell

Choose the correct spelling. Write it on the line.

1. Will you hepp/**help** us feed the chickens? — help
2. The feed is in the **bern**/barn. — barn
3. Nowe/**Now** we get the eggs. — Now
4. Then we can drive to **town**/tone. — town

Circle two words in each row that rhyme with the first word.

1.	down	(gown)	(town)	done
2.	farm	(charm)	ham	(harm)
3.	brown	brow	(clown)	(crown)
4.	now	low	(cow)	(how)

Our Farm

Mark an X on the misspelled words. Spell them correctly on the lines.

1. Sam lives on a fram. — farm
2. Sam has a kow. — cow
3. We will go done to see his cow. — down
4. She is broun with a white face. — brown

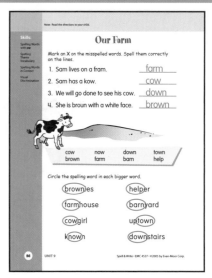

| cow | now | down | town |
| brown | farm | barn | help |

Circle the spelling word in each bigger word.

(brown)ies — (helper)
(farm)house — (barn)yard
(cow)girl — up(town)
(known) — (down)stairs

Finish the Sentences

▶ A sentence that tells something ends with a period. (.)
We are going to the farm.

A sentence that asks something ends with a question mark. (?)
Would you like to visit a farm?

Fill in the blanks with words from the box below. End each sentence with a period or a question mark.

1. Our friends live on a farm.
2. Have you ever been inside a red barn?
3. They have horses, pigs, and a cow.
4. Do you live on a farm or in town?
5. Is your horse black or brown?
6. Let's go to town now.

| farm | now | barn | town | brown | cow |

Contractions

A contraction is a short way to write two words. A contraction uses an apostrophe. (')

We will plant the beans.
We'll plant corn, too.

Write the contraction for each pair of words. Use an apostrophe.

1. you will — you'll
2. I am — I'm
3. here is — here's
4. you are — you're
5. is not — isn't
6. we have — we've
7. what is — what's
8. did not — didn't

Is and Are

▶ Use **is** with one and **are** with more than one.

The pear is in the basket.
The apples are in the box.

Fill in each blank with is or are.

1. Our farm is a fruit farm.
2. That tree is a pear tree.
3. The pears are ready to pick.
4. There are boxes for the pears.
5. Here is the pear truck.
6. The apple trees are over there.
7. This is a sweet apple.
8. The apples are in a basket.

Farm Questions

Think of three facts you know about farms. Write each fact as a question. End each question with a question mark.

1. Answers will vary.
2.
3.

Draw a picture of a farm.

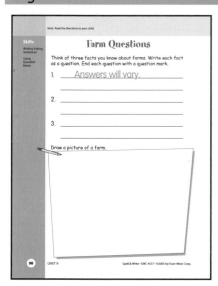

On the Farm

Write a story about a class trip to a farm. Tell what the children saw. Use as many spelling words as you can.

| cow | now | down | town |
| brown | farm | barn | help |

Answers will vary.

✓ Check Your Story
○ I used complete sentences.
○ I used a period or question mark at the end of each sentence.

TEST YOUR SKILLS On the Farm

Find the correct answer. Fill in the circle.

1. Which punctuation mark goes at the end of the sentence?
Do you live on a farm___
○ period (.)
● question mark (?)

2. Which word is the contraction for **did not**?
○ don't
● didn't

3. Which word goes in the sentence?
These ___ the pears we picked.
○ is
● are

4. Write the sentence correctly.
does the brawn kow stay in the bran
Does the brown cow stay in the barn?

My Spelling Test
Ask someone to test you on the spelling words.

1.
2.
3.
4.
5.
6.
7.
8.

Pet Show

We are having a pet show today. Nick will bring a little bunny. It is black and white.

Sierra will bring her kitten. The kitten has a bell that always tells where she is.

I will bring my funny puppy to the pet show. His name is Tucker. I am teaching Tucker to sit. He is happy when he gets a treat. He wags his tail and licks my face.

Can you come to our pet show?

Find It! Read the spelling words. Check off the words you can find in the story.

✓ funny ✓ bunny ✓ puppy ✓ happy
✓ little ✓ kitten ✓ pet ✓ my

How many spelling words did you find? 8

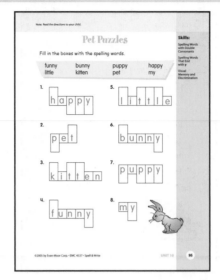

Pet Puzzles

Fill in the boxes with the spelling words.

funny bunny puppy happy
little kitten pet my

1. h a p p y
2. p e t
3. k i t t e n
4. f u n n y
5. l i t t l e
6. b u n n y
7. p u p p y
8. m y

Skills:
Spelling Words with Double Consonants
Spelling Words That End with y
Visual Memory and Discrimination

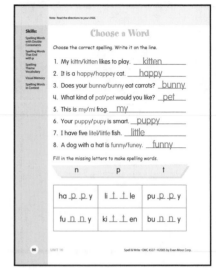

Choose a Word

Choose the correct spelling. Write it on the line.

1. My kittn/kitten likes to play. kitten
2. It is a happy/happey cat. happy
3. Does your bunne/bunny eat carrots? bunny
4. What kind of pat/pet would you like? pet
5. This is my/mi frog. my
6. Your puppy/pupy is smart. puppy
7. I have five litel/little fish. little
8. A dog with a hat is funny/funey. funny

Fill in the missing letters to make spelling words.

n   p   t

| ha p p y | li t t le | pu p p y |
| fu n n y | ki t t en | bu n n y |

Skills:
Spelling Words with Double Consonants
Spelling Words That End with y
Spelling Theme Vocabulary
Visual Memory
Spelling Words in Context

Correct Capitals

A sentence begins with a capital letter.

My dog takes me for a walk.

Circle the sentences that begin with a capital letter. Fix the letters that should be capitals.

1. My kitten is a good pet.
2. It likes to play with a ball of string.
3. The funny kitten got twisted up.
4. I had to help it.
5. Now my kitten is happy.
6. What does your puppy play with?
7. Does the bunny like to play?
8. Every pet needs love.

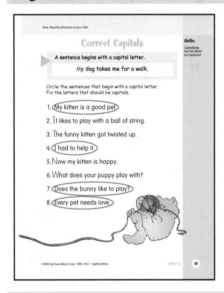

Skills:
Capitalizing the First Word in a Sentence

Capitals for Names

Skills:
Capitalizing Names of People, Pets, and Specific Places and Things

The names of people, pets, and specific places and things begin with a capital letter.

April has two horses named Hanna and Harry.
She rides at Oak Tree Ranch.

Use red to circle the names of people and pets. Use blue to circle the names of special places and things.

1. Today the Texas State Fair begins.
2. April will take her horse.
3. She will brush Hanna's coat.
4. Carlos comes from Red River Ranch.
5. Carlos will ride in the ring.
6. He will ride a horse named Rex.
7. April and Carlos want a blue ribbon.
8. The blue ribbon says First Place.

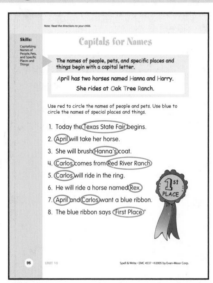

Pick Your Pronoun

Skills:
Using Pronouns

Some words take the place of names. These words are called pronouns.

Bunny Boo likes to hop around the yard.
She hops in the grass.

Fill in the blanks with words from the box below. Replace the underlined words.

1. My dog Trotter is a fast runner.
   He likes to play chase.
2. My kittens are Pepper and Spice.
   They look alike.
3. Tina and I have pet birds.
   The birds sing to us.
4. Mom and I want a puppy.
   We want a little one.

we   he   us   they

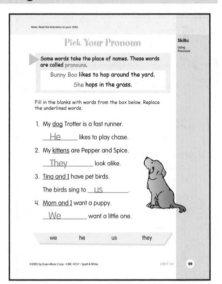

Skills:
Writing Complete Sentences
Capitalizing the First Word in a Sentence

Pet Report

Answer the questions using complete sentences. Use a capital letter at the beginning of each sentence.

1. What pet would you choose?
   Answers will vary.

2. Why would you choose that pet?

3. What is a good name for your pet?

Draw a picture of your pet.

Make a Poster

The children are having a pet show. Make a sign for the show. Decorate your sign. How many spelling words can you use?

funny bunny puppy happy
little kitten pet my

Drawings will vary.

Skills:
Creative Writing
Writing Information
Making a Poster

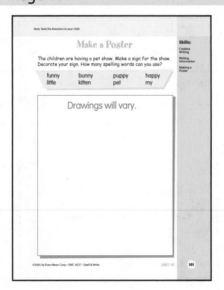

TEST YOUR SKILLS Pet Show

Find the correct answer. Fill in the circle.

1. Which sentence has the correct capital letter?
   ○ the pet show is today.
   ● I like the kittens.

2. Which sentence has the correct capital letters?
   ● My dog went to Red's Puppy School.
   ○ now clifford knows how to sit.

3. Which pronoun goes in the blank?
   Luke has a new kitten.
   ____ calls it Penny.
   ● He
   ○ They

4. Write the sentence correctly.
   mi littel bunny is named sunny
   My little bunny is named Sunny.

My Spelling Test
Ask someone to test you on the spelling words.

1. _____
2. _____
3. _____
4. _____
5. _____
6. _____
7. _____
8. _____

Page 103

Page 105

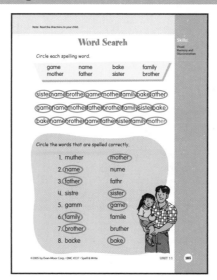

Page 106

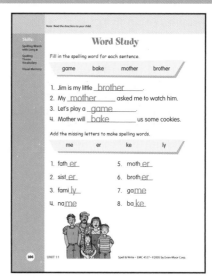

Page 107

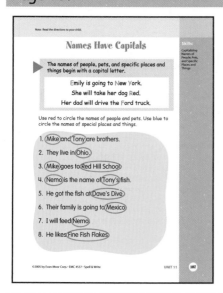

Page 108

Page 109

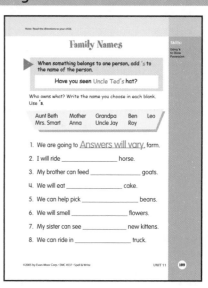

Page 110

Page 111

Page 112

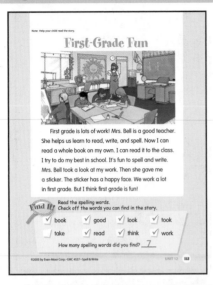

First-Grade Fun

First grade is lots of work! Mrs. Bell is a good teacher. She helps us learn to read, write, and spell. Now I can read a whole book on my own. I can read it to the class. I try to do my best in school. It's fun to spell and write. Mrs. Bell took a look at my work. Then she gave me a sticker. The sticker has a happy face. We work a lot in first grade. But I think first grade is fun!

Find It! Read the spelling words. Check off the words you can find in the story.

☑ book ☑ good ☑ look ☑ took
☐ take ☑ read ☑ think ☑ work

How many spelling words did you find? _7_

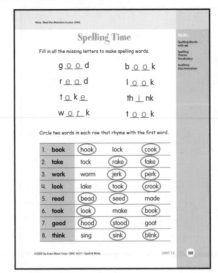

Spelling Time

Fill in all the missing letters to make spelling words.

g o o d   b o o k
r e a d   l o o k
t a k e   th i nk
w o r k   t o o k

Circle two words in each row that rhyme with the first word.

1. book — (hook) lock (cook)
2. take — tock (rake) (fake)
3. work — worm (jerk) (perk)
4. look — lake (took) (crook)
5. read — (bead) (seed) made
6. took — (look) make (book)
7. good — (hood) (stood) goat
8. think — sing (sink) (blink)

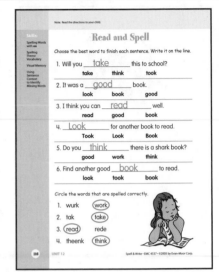

Read and Spell

Choose the best word to finish each sentence. Write it on the line.

1. Will you __take__ this to school?
   take think took
2. It was a __good__ book.
   look book good
3. I think you can __read__ well.
   read good book
4. __Look__ for another book to read.
   Took Look Book
5. Do you __think__ there is a shark book?
   good work think
6. Find another good __book__ to read.
   look took book

Circle the words that are spelled correctly.

1. wurk (work)
2. tak (take)
3. (read) rede
4. theenk (think)

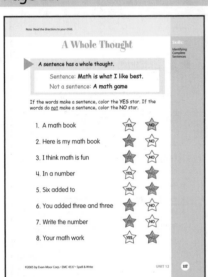

A Whole Thought

A sentence has a whole thought.

Sentence: Math is what I like best.
Not a sentence: A math game

If the words make a sentence, color the YES star. If the words do not make a sentence, color the NO star.

1. A math book — NO
2. Here is my math book — YES
3. I think math is fun — YES
4. In a number — NO
5. Six added to — NO
6. You added three and three — YES
7. Write the number — YES
8. Your math work — NO

Make It a Capital

The names of people, pets, and specific places and things begin with a capital letter.

We go to Big Creek School.
Mr. King is the music teacher.
We sing "America the Beautiful."

Cross out the words that do not need a capital letter.

Teacher	Miss Pool	First Street School
School	Boston	City
Book	Iowa	State
Song	Helper	Mrs. Pine
Mr. Sims	Bus Driver	Curious George

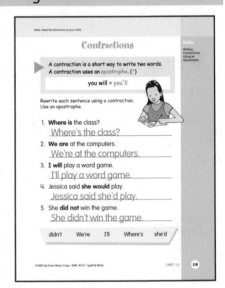

Contractions

A contraction is a short way to write two words. A contraction uses an apostrophe. (')

you will = you'll

Rewrite each sentence using a contraction. Use an apostrophe.

1. **Where is** the class?
   Where's the class?
2. **We are** at the computers.
   We're at the computers.
3. **I will** play a word game.
   I'll play a word game.
4. Jessica said **she would** play.
   Jessica said she'd play.
5. She **did not** win the game.
   She didn't win the game.

didn't   We're   I'll   Where's   she'd

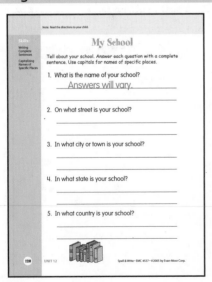

My School

Tell about your school. Answer each question with a complete sentence. Use capitals for names of specific places.

1. What is the name of your school?
   Answers will vary.
2. On what street is your school?
3. In what city or town is your school?
4. In what state is your school?
5. In what country is your school?

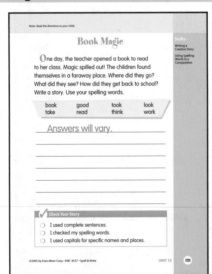

Book Magic

One day, the teacher opened a book to read to her class. Magic spilled out! The children found themselves in a faraway place. Where did they go? What did they see? How did they get back to school? Write a story. Use your spelling words.

| book | good | took | look |
| take | read | think | work |

Answers will vary.

Check Your Story
○ I used complete sentences.
○ I checked my spelling words.
○ I used capitals for specific names and places.

TEST YOUR SKILLS — First-Grade Fun

Find the correct answer. Fill in the circle.

1. Which one is a sentence?
   ○ Your book
   ● I like your book
2. Which sentence has the correct capital letters?
   ○ Our School is in california.
   ● Their school is in Texas.
3. Which word is the contraction for **you are**?
   ○ you'll
   ● you're

4. Write the sentence correctly.
   she didnt werk at lincoln school
   She didn't work at Lincoln School.

My Spelling Test

Ask someone to test you on the spelling words.

1. _____
2. _____
3. _____
4. _____
5. _____
6. _____
7. _____
8. _____